WildBlue
TRUE CRIME
features

JOHN FERAK

DIXIE'S LAST STAND

WAS IT **MURDER** OR **SELF-DEFENSE**?

WildBlue Press

WildBluePress.com

Dixie's Last Stand published by:

WILDBLUE PRESS

1153 Bergen Pkwy Ste I #114

Evergreen, Colorado 80439

eBook ISBN: 978-1-942266-07-5

Trade Paperback ISBN: 978-1-942266-12-9

ACKNOWLEDGMENTS

Lots of people were instrumental in helping me recreate and comprise the factual events involved with the Dixie Shanahan murder case.

First, special praise goes out to WildBlue Press co-founders Steve Jackson and Michael Cordova, for launching a true-crime book publishing company that is like no other publishing firm. Special recognition also goes to book designer Elijah Toten and copy editor Jenni Grubbs for their outstanding hard work and careful attention to detail during the final stages of production for DIXIE'S LAST STAND.

Along those lines, I would like to extend a special thanks to those of you who are devoted and faithful readers of true-crime. I know I speak for the other authors at WildBlue Press in offering my sincerest gratitude and deepest appreciation for those of you who take the time to read our books. Without you, there simply would be no reason to research and produce our books.

In addition, I would like to single out true-crime author RJ Parker for truly going above the call of duty to help promote DIXIE'S LAST STAND amongst RJ's army of true-crime followers across the world. If you are not reading a true-crime book published by WildBlue Press, please consider reading one of the many fine true-crime books authored by RJ Parker, including one of his latest, "Serial Killer Groupies."

Others who were instrumental in the production and presentation of DIXIE'S LAST STAND:

Terry O'Grady, a courts reporter in Iowa, was responsible for transcribing the entire court proceedings regarding the case involving Dixie Shanahan. Many of the direct quotations that were used in this true-crime book were contained within the official court transcripts taken during State v. Dixie Lynn Shanahan as transcribed by O'Grady. These quotations took place during Dixie Shanahan's pretrial motion hearings, during her jury trial or at her sentencing hearing. Other direct quotations contained within the book were derived from a number of interviews that I conducted with key persons. There were a few occasions where I included direct quotations from past newspaper articles that I had written for the Omaha World-Herald; others are duly noted within the book as coming from various news media outlets.

Carol Hunter, executive news editor at the Des Moines Register, graciously took the time to furnish me with access to several high-quality photos contained within the Des Moines Register's archives. Carol actually hired me — and my future wife, Andrea — back in 2000 when she was the executive editor of the Green

Bay Press-Gazette in Wisconsin. Carol also attended our wedding two years later. I left the Green Bay paper in late 2003 to become a journalist in Omaha, and within a few years Carol moved over to the Des Moines Register to become an editor there. These days, our family is back in Wisconsin. I work out of the Post-Crescent in Appleton as the investigative team editor for Gannett Wisconsin Media.

Bob Bjoin, managing editor of the Harlan Iowa Newspapers, provided access to several of his newspaper's high-quality archived photographs to republish for DIXIE'S LAST STAND. Just like the Register, the Harlan Newspapers also provided excellent news coverage for its readers in covering the murder case involving Dixie Shanahan.

Fred Scaletta, assistant director of Iowa Department of Corrections, was diligent and extremely helpful in facilitating my requests for public information related to Dixie Shanahan.

Also, a special thank-you to: retired Shelby County Sheriff Gene Cavenaugh and his successor, Sheriff Mark Hervey; Joe Jordan, managing editor of Nebraska Watchdog; Charles Thoman, retired assistant attorney general for the State of Iowa; and now-retired Iowa District Judge Charles Smith III for taking the time to allow me to interview them. Their first-hand insight was invaluable.

My wonderful wife, Andrea, who has developed quite a knack for coming up with the clever true-crime book titles. Andrea suggested the title of DIXIE'S

LAST STAND for this true-crime feature. When her proposed title was crowd-sourced by WildBlue Press with four other possible book titles, readers chose her title by overwhelming fashion. (She also came up with the title for my first book, which came out in June 2014, BLOODY LIES: A CSI SCANDAL IN THE HEARTLAND.)

DIXIE'S LAST STAND: WAS IT MURDER OR SELF-DEFENSE? *Is dedicated to those small-town law enforcement investigators who vigorously pursue the truth and justice even when constrained by circumstances and very limited resources.*

Preface — That Window

It was a cold, blustery afternoon in the middle of December in western Iowa. It was time for Robert McConnell to make his rounds reading the town's water meters. Normally, McConnell worked as a painter. He had lived in Defiance, Iowa, since the mid-1970s. He had read the little town's water meters for three years. He liked the routine and was highly efficient.

Just like clockwork, McConnell walked the town every fifteenth day of the month. And it barely took him three hours to complete the task. Nobody would confuse Defiance with Iowa's largest metropolitan city of Des Moines.

Defiance was a cozy, sleepy bedroom community about sixty miles northeast of downtown Omaha, Nebraska. Defiance had three hundred forty-six residents during the 2000 census.

Besides the post office and city hall, there weren't a lot of buildings in the heart of town to lure in daytime visitors. During weekdays, it was rare to find more than a few vehicles parked along Defiance's main drag. Most residents flocked to the neighboring cities of Denison or Harlan to work or to shop. On weekends in Defiance, the hot spot where locals came to unwind was a tavern called Tobe's Place. People drank tap beer, ate grilled burgers, and swapped the latest small-town gossip around rural Shelby County, Iowa.

One of the homes on McConnell's meter-reading route was a well-kept ranch with a large yard that encompassed two acres. Several large evergreens and shade trees gave the property a secluded feel. Built around 1980, the gray-colored ranch once belonged to the late Al and Beverly Feser. After Bev died in 1994, her only child, Scott Shanahan, inherited her home. By 2002, he lived there with his wife, Dixie, and their two young children.

But back during the winter of 2002, McConnell noticed something odd and peculiar when he wandered onto the Shanahans' property to read their water meter tucked in the corner of their backyard. It was one of the back windows, in the northeast corner of the home.

"The window was totally open," McConnell said.

If this were Orlando, Atlanta, or Phoenix, having an open window in the middle of December would be no big deal. But Defiance, Iowa, was in the midst of a typical Midwestern winter. This meant plenty of snow and frigid temperatures over the course of several months.

Actually, McConnell first noticed the wide open back

bedroom window when he made his regular meter-reading rounds around November 15, 2002.

"But then the next month in December, it was still open. January, it was still open. February, it was still open," McConnell remembered.

Sometime early in the spring of 2003, someone closed that window shut. And the window stayed shut during the rest of the year.

Chapter 1 — Rumors

Defiance, Iowa, is so small that the community does not have its own police force. Residents must rely upon the services of the Shelby County Sheriff's Office, about twelve miles away in the county seat of Harlan. Photo courtesy of The Des Moines Register

Veteran Shelby County Sheriff's Deputy John Kelly rolled his cruiser out of the county seat in Harlan,

Iowa. He passed countless rows of tall cornfields and plenty of rustic barns during his fifteen-minute drive north along U.S. Route 59. Inevitably, a large brown sign proclaimed, "Welcome to Defiance." There, Kelly slowed his squad car and turned into the sleepy western Iowa town. Like most small-town cops, Kelly was a jack-of-all trades. He responded to crashes and scouted for speeders and motorists who were disobeying traffic laws. He conducted criminal investigations. He also was a firearms instructor. And with twenty-six years of experience on the sheriff's department, Kelly was quite familiar with the names and faces of folks residing around Shelby County, Iowa, notably those in the quaint and friendly small towns.

With barely a hundred residential rooftops in Defiance, it did not take Kelly long to find his destination that summer afternoon on July 22, 2003. The gray-colored ranch at 206 Third Avenue already had been a frequent hot spot for the Shelby County Sheriff's office in recent years. Homeowner Scott Shanahan had been a frequent flyer in the Shelby County Jail. Scott had been arrested three separate times by the Shelby County deputies from 1997 to 2000. All three episodes involved explosive and hideous incidents of domestic violence. Because of those interactions with Scott Shanahan, sheriff's deputies also were well acquainted with his often bruised and battered wife named Dixie. By the summer of 2003, the Defiance couple was raising three young children. Their youngest child, a baby girl, was just born that March.

As soon as the deputy parked in the driveway, Dixie Shanahan ran outside. She met the sheriff's deputy on the sidewalk, near the front bay window. Dixie wasn't in a friendly mood. She was curious why Kelly had the nerve of pulling into her driveway. She thought the cop's appearance during the middle of the day would surely create a stir around the small-town rumor mill. Unbeknownst to her, rumors were the primary reason why Shelby County Sheriff's Deputy Kelly had dropped in at Dixie's residence to speak with her in the first place.

"There had been rumors that had been brought to the sheriff's attention that Scott was missing," Kelly told her.

Dixie reacted by claiming she had not seen her no-good husband for an entire year. She guessed that she last saw him sometime the previous August. The last time the couple supposedly spoke was over the phone roughly six months ago, she told Kelly.

In that situation, Scott had called, demanding that he be present in the hospital delivery room to witness the birth of their third child. "Dixie said that she told him that he would not be present," Kelly stated. "She would fight to keep him from being there while the baby was born."

Indeed, Scott was a no-show for the March 2003 birth of his little girl. And after that, he made no further attempts to contact Dixie. He never once tried to see his newborn baby at any point in 2003. He never tried to visit any of his three children for that matter.

And yet, Scott Shanahan's brown, Ford pickup truck remained parked in his driveway. It was as if Scott hadn't left the house.

Chapter 2 — Doomed Marriage

Denison, Iowa, has a large water tower that hovers over the community proclaiming, "It's a Wonderful Life." This western Iowa city of about 7,300 sits at the crossroads of U.S. Highways 30 and 59. Denison boasts that it is the proud hometown of famous Hollywood movie actress Donna Reed, who played Mary Hatch in the 1946 Hollywood classic alongside Jimmy Stewart.

Scott Shanahan also was born in Denison on December 14, 1962, but his was not a wonderful life. He grew into a mean and nasty little runt. With brown hair and brown eyes, he stood 5-foot-4 and weighed 155 pounds.

During the 1980s, Scott Shanahan worked for a few years in Oakland, Iowa, at Oakland Beef. But he was not the most reliable and dependable guy. He lacked the discipline to stay focused and keep a job. In 2000, he worked very briefly at the Quality Machine Inc., in Audubon, Iowa, but the business owner fired him because he just wasn't showing up for work.

And that was Scott Shanahan, a small-town deadbeat and jobless slacker. His wife, Dixie, wasn't exactly sympathetic and content with her husband's decision to just stay home and be a bum.

"He had this shop and he did work on cars, but not as a job," Dixie said. "Not ever as a job."

Most people who knew Scott Shanahan would say he did not have his priorities straight. Scott was fond of sleeping in bed until noon. When he got up, he spent his time restoring classic cars and tractors in his garage across the street from his home on Third Avenue. Townsfolk knew all too well that Scott was very possessive of his autos and his mechanic's tools. The wise ones just left Scott alone and stayed away from him.

There was one rather memorable occasion when Dixie confronted him about getting a job and earning a paycheck to help pay the bills.

"I told him he needed to get a job and work on these (cars) as a hobby," Dixie said. "He ultimately stuck my head in the toilet, and he told me he was going to flush my head down the toilet, and my children seen this. He went off on me again by beating me, saying he had his priorities straight."

It turns out that Scott wasn't just possessive of his autos. He was possessive of everything. He was regarded as a control freak and a genuine jerk. Above all, he was possessive of his wife, Dixie, his family, and his family's financial affairs. Scott also was a gun nut. He kept about a dozen different firearms around his home, mostly to intimidate and terrify his passive wife. She didn't have the faintest clue how to operate a gun, let alone properly load the ammunition shells into one of his shotguns.

For the longest time, Scott mercilessly beat his wife for lots of pathetic and disgusting reasons. One time, he gave her a black eye and ranted around town about their boring sex life. He even had the gall to tell some of Dixie's girlfriends that they should give her pointers to be better in the sack.

"That they ought to teach me how to be better in bed because I was terrible in bed," Dixie recalled. "That I was no good, that I was worthless."

On another occasion, Dixie cooked mashed potatoes on her stove for her family for supper. Scott absolutely hated the mashed potatoes. He then went berserk on her.

"He came in and told me that they was God awful, that they was too runny," Dixie explained.

Scott grabbed the dinner plate. He busted the ceramic over Dixie's noggin. He made her clean up the mess that he caused.

Susan Holm had lived in one of the homes that brushed up against Scott and Dixie Shanahan's large backyard in Defiance. One day in her backyard, Holm heard Scott spewing profanity all the way from inside his home. The noises sounded so awful inside the Shanahan home that Holm whisked her ten-year-old son inside. The boy had been playing in the backyard. Susan Holm did not want his ears subjected to the awful domestic spat taking place across their property line.

Holm presumed that Scott was screaming at Dixie.

"He was yelling at another person calling them dirty names, cunt, whore, any nasty word that you could think of came out of his mouth," Susan Holm said. "It sounded almost like … they were fighting and something hitting, a loud thud against what sounded like glass. Screaming in pain, what sounded like pain."

And then, there was the time when Scott ordered his wife to buy all the cement-making mix to pour a concrete sidewalk toward the front entrance of their house. She wound up driving to several neighboring towns to acquire the right mix. Unfortunately, the cement mix she bought turned out too runny.

"This ain't gonna work!" Scott growled. "You're going to do it. I'm not doing it."

Poor Dixie had to pour the cement sidewalk by herself.

"I had no clue what I was doing," Dixie said.

Her husband could have cared less. After all, it was another episode where Scott had a chance to mock and humiliate her.

"Well, if it don't work, you're going to be the one jack-hammering it out," he snarled.

Mad, Scott Shanahan grabbed a pair of hedge clippers and threw them at her.

* * *

Dixie's difficult life revolved around fear. She feared her husband. She feared for her children's safety. She feared telling anybody about being subjected to regular beatings by the hands of her unloving husband. Scott Shanahan often beat her up two or three times a week.

Then, one day, Dixie finally worked up some courage.

On May 31, 1997, she placed a phone call to the Shelby County Sheriff's Office twelve miles away in Harlan. Like most of the communities in Shelby County, Defiance was way too small to operate its own police force. The residents here relied upon the diligent sheriff's office in the county seat of Harlan for help.

Indeed, sheriff's deputies were dispatched to the Shanahan home on Third Avenue to investigate her call. Upon arrival, Dixie explained that her husband had beaten her as they had driven back from Council Bluffs, a city about fifty-five miles south of Defiance. Her eyes were bruised. Her lips were bloodied.

"He ended up punching me in the side of the face, banging my head into the door of the glass on the car," Dixie recalled.

The Shelby County Sheriff's Office was a small agency. It consisted of less than ten sworn officers, including longtime Sheriff Gene Cavenaugh. The deputies were competent, courteous, and acted with the utmost professionalism. Dixie also relayed to the deputies that her pounding on the ride home from Council Bluffs that day had not been the first time she had been assaulted by her violent husband. Sheriff's deputies put Scott Shanahan in handcuffs and stuffed him into the back of the squad car.

Back in Harlan, Scott was thrown in the Shelby County Jail. The jail was quite small. The facility only had enough room to house a dozen male prisoners and two female inmates.

Rather quickly, Scott Shanahan was able to post bail. His misdemeanor criminal case proceeded along on the criminal docket over at the Shelby County Courthouse down the street in the middle of the downtown square. By the time Scott Shanahan decided to enter his guilty plea, his battered and abused wife had now come to his defense. The sentencing judge gave Scott thirty days in jail, but Scott caught a lucky break. The judge decided to suspend twenty-eight of those days in jail. In a nutshell, Scott Shanahan only had to serve two days in jail for his shameful and unconscionable behavior of beating his defenseless wife, Dixie. The judge, did, however, put Scott on probation for two years. Scott was ordered to undergo counseling and attend a domestic batterer's education program.

The judge was hopeful that Scott Shanahan would change his ways.

So was Dixie.

She went ahead and wrote a letter to the judge begging him to lift the restraining order that had been previously placed on her husband following his arrest for domestic violence.

"I Dixie Shanahan would like the restraining order lifted against my husband Scott Shanahan because I am no longer afraid that he will hurt me and I would like to keep my marriage together and with the restraining order this is not possible to try. He is in counciling (sic) now and I feel this is helping him. We have a 9 month old son so if at all possible I would like this lifted so we can work this out." Signed by Dixie Shanahan, July 2, 1997

If Scott Shanahan changed his ways, it didn't last long.

On July 27, Scott grew violent. Their marriage was over, he shouted. He told Dixie she had exactly five seconds to get out of their house. He began counting. One, two, three, four, and five. But she hadn't left. Scott was furious. He clutched her arm. He hauled her straight into the garage. This time, she tried to stand up to him. She threatened to call the police on him. Scott went berserk. He fumed and grabbed his wife by her long, dark hair. "I will show you what happens when you call the sheriff," Scott yelled as he drilled his wife back and forth with his fists. Before long, Dixie's head also bled. Eventually, Scott used a long metal object to strike both her legs. When the beatings were over, Scott went around the house and unplugged their landline phones. He wanted to be damn sure that Dixie had no way to call the sheriff's office.

At that moment, Dixie Shanahan felt helpless and trapped. Her body ached. Her pain was intense. She did not call the Shelby County law enforcement that particular day.

Then, about six weeks later, Dixie had had enough.

She worked up the strength to make the twelve-mile drive into Harlan. She drove through the downtown and through the vibrant downtown square that consisted of several retail shops, a few restaurants, and a handful of professional offices, including some law firms. She parked in front of the Shelby County Sheriff's Office. She strode inside and filed a formal police report about the July 27 domestic abuse. Dixie was at ease and no longer afraid.

She candidly told sheriff's deputies that her husband controlled her every waking move. This marked the first time in six weeks that she finally felt safe to sneak away from her Defiance home to contact law enforcement. But she also feared the consequences. As fate would have it, Dixie was pregnant and carrying Scott's second child. Would Scott Shanahan take away her baby, if he knew she was accusing him of committing more domestic abuse?

Even though Dixie was pregnant, Scott continued to beat her. She was deathly afraid that Scott might turn one of his guns on her. This time, she notified the sheriff's office that her explosively violent husband kept several guns within their home.

Just like the first time, the Shelby County Sheriff's Office took Dixie's domestic violence accusations seriously. This time, Scott Shanahan was arrested for second-degree abusive assault.

Now that Scott was in jail again, Dixie had complete freedom. But being alone and away from Scott wasn't what she wanted. In the coming days, Dixie wanted Scott back in her life. She wanted him back. She pleaded with the Shelby County judicial system to grant mercy to her abusive and dangerous husband. She wrote another letter to the court system. This letter was dated Feb. 10, 1998.

"To whom it may concern: This letter is concerning the domestic abuse case against Scott Shanahan. I would like the charges against him dismissed. I know he has been attending his BEP classes as required and also on his own has been seeing a councler (sic) and a psychiatrist so he is making every effort to get help. I cannot see where jail time would be beneficial to him at all. In all fairness, some of the things I said were exaggerated and this whole thing has been blown out of proportion. As for federal weapons charges I really feel this is unfair because it was only a few weeks before the incident that we were aware of this... Please take this letter into consideration in the above matter and resolve this issue." Sincerely, Dixie Shanahan.

Wisely, prosecutors in the Shelby County Attorney's Office did not heed Dixie's advice. The domestic abuse charges facing Scott Shanahan were not dismissed as Dixie had desired.

On Feb. 23, 1998, Scott Shanahan was convicted of second-degree domestic abuse assault. Although the sentencing judge gave him two years in prison, the incarceration was suspended. Instead, Scott Shanahan was ordered to serve a total of four days in the county jail, pay a one-thousand-dollar fine, and, once again, attend a domestic violence batterers' program. The sentencing judge also placed him under court probation for a year.

But, there was one part of the judge's sentence that Scott Shanahan absolutely hated. The judge ordered him to surrender his firearms to the Shelby County Sheriff's Office. Scott was told to dispose of all his firearms and give the sales' proceeds to charity.

But Scott didn't want to part with any of his beloved guns. He loved his guns a lot more than he cared for his wife. In the coming days, Scott went out and contacted his uncle Dean Feser, who also lived in Defiance. Dean Feser was familiar with Scott as a young boy, but the two hadn't had much contact during the past twenty years.

"He wanted somebody to hang onto his guns because he said he could get them back in five years," Feser said. "He told me in five years, if he keeps his nose clean, he can get them back."

It turned out that Scott Shanahan had quite a weapons cache. He had an automatic shotgun, a few pump shotguns, including a .410 pump, a .243

high-powered rifle, plus various pistols. Dean Feser estimated there might have been nine guns in all.

Inevitably, Dean Feser began to second-guess his initial decision to safe harbor his abusive nephew's collection of firearms. After all, his troubled nephew had multiple arrests for domestic violence. Wondering what to do, Dean Feser sought advice from Sheriff Gene Cavenaugh. Was it OK to be safe-keeping those dangerous weapons knowing full well that Scott Shanahan continued to run afoul of the law?

The sheriff strongly urged the Defiance man not to give those weapons back to Scott Shanahan.

"And he said bring them down, and he'll lock them up in the safe," Feser remembered.

Feser figured his options were to give the guns over to the sheriff or sell them outright.

He called Scott Shanahan to discuss the matter. Not surprisingly, his nephew was adamant that the guns not be turned over to the Shelby County Sheriff's Office under any circumstances. So, Dean Feser went ahead and instead sold off Scott's weapons. He wanted to put the proceeds into a college savings account for Scott and Dixie's two young children.

But, those noble efforts by Scott's uncle hit a giant brick wall. For starters, Scott Shanahan refused to believe that his law-abiding uncle had actually sold off Scott's firearms.

As time marched on, Scott grew more and more agitated and perturbed with his uncle. Scott convinced himself that his uncle had lied to him. Scott continued to pester his uncle, demanding that the middle-aged man return Scott's rightful weapons.

One day, the tense situation came to a climax. Scott parked his pickup truck in front of his uncle's residence. He walked up to the door and confronted his uncle with pure anger.

"Where's my guns?" Scott barked.

"They're gone," Dean Feser responded.

Then, Feser asked his nephew to furnish him with the Social Security numbers for Scott's children. Feser wanted to make good on his promise to deposit the money from the guns sales into a bank account for them. He didn't want Scott Shanahan to use the money for booze, drugs, or personal pleasure.

Scott grew boisterous. The men exchanged words. Scott threatened to call the sheriff. Dean Feser ordered his hot-headed nephew to get off his property at once. No punches were thrown that day. Scott left the property. He was mad and empty-handed.

Sure enough, that was not the last confrontation between irate Scott the bum and his easygoing, law-abiding uncle.

The real showdown was still weeks away.

One afternoon, Scott noticed his uncle out hauling

grain for a local farmer. Scott parked his truck along the highway. It was time to confront his uncle about those firearms that Scott was absolutely convinced were being hidden from him.

"Where is my guns?" Scott shouted.

"They're gone," his uncle responded truthfully.

Again, Scott refused to believe that his uncle got rid of his weapons.

Words were exchanged. Tensions simmered.

"He threatened to put me in jail and call the lawyer," Feser recalled.

By that point, Dean Feser had grown sick and tired of his lazy, good-for-nothing, volatile nephew. He was tired of being badgered by Scott about the firearms cache.

Dean Feser, a normally mild-mannered Defiance man, punched his own nephew right in the gut.

"I smacked him one," Feser said.

Scott whimpered back across the highway toward his truck. As he retreated, Scott cursed at his uncle and threatened to put him in jail before the end of the night.

"You're going to hear from my lawyer," Scott shouted.

Feser could care less about his lousy, jobless nephew's

veiled threats. Unlike his worthless nephew, he needed to focus his attention on his work.

That afternoon, Dean Feser busily continued to haul away grain, since it was harvest time.

Chapter 3 — Early Years

How Dixie and Scott Shanahan ever ended up married was a twisted, cruel, and tangled web of wicked fate.

Dixie Schrieber was born in 1967 in Muscatine, Iowa, to Richard and Darlene Schrieber. Dixie had two brothers and two sisters. However, her father died when Dixie was less than three years old. Her mother soon remarried, and that was bad news for Dixie and her sisters. Her new stepfather was sexually abusive, and he molested Dixie and her sisters, she testified, years later. Dixie estimated that the sexual abuse lasted for about a decade.

As the sexual abuse persisted, the family moved a lot. That also made it harder for the police to keep tabs on any allegations and suspicions of child neglect and sexual abuse within the home. Dixie's family bounced from Muscatine to Denison, Iowa, and eventually, they crossed the Missouri River and moved to Yutan, Nebraska, a small farming town on the far western fringe of Omaha.

Scott and Dixie Shanahan lived in this ranch house in Defiance, Iowa. Scott inherited the home following his mother's death in 1994. Photo courtesy of The Des Moines Register

In 1984, at age seventeen, Dixie made a decision that would change the course of her life. She broke free from her sick and pathetic, sexually abusive stepfather.

"I confronted him and told him that I was going to go to the police, and my stepfather ended up leaving with another woman that was staying at our house because he was afraid that I was going to go to the police," Dixie said.

Dixie had already settled on a place to go.

It was a cozy ranch tucked in the middle of a tiny Iowa town. The address was 206 Third Avenue. The home belonged to Beverly and Al Feser. This was quite convenient because Dixie had started dating their son the previous year, 1983, when she was sixteen and he was twenty-one.

The young man's name was Scott Shanahan.

Scott Shanahan was born in Denison, Iowa, but spent nearly his entire life in nearby Defiance. Photo courtesy of Shelby County Sheriff's Office

"My mother asked Scott's mom if I could stay there," Dixie said.

The request was granted by Scott's mother. Dixie had permission to move into the Fesers' home.

This was where Dixie would live for the next twenty years.

Dixie adjusted quite well to her change of scenery. The Fesers kind of became her adopted family. But, Al Feser had serious health problems. Diabetes left him with both his legs amputated. He also was legally blind. "He couldn't see things, so of course I would help him get things and help him do the things he needed to," Dixie said.

Mrs. Feser wasn't in the best of health, either.

She had suffered a heart attack and underwent a triple bypass during the mid-1980s. To help out, Dixie drove Mrs. Feser to the grocery store and ran errands for her. In 1988, Mrs. Feser suffered a serious bout of pneumonia. The lingering illness required the woman to remain on an oxygen tank twenty-four hours a day. Over time, Dixie and the woman developed a special bond.

"She was more like my mother than my own mother," Dixie said.

In any event, Dixie had fallen in love with Bev and Al's only son. But, Dixie saw signs of storm clouds over the horizon. Her older boyfriend showed quite a mean streak toward his parents. Oftentimes, Scott bickered with his mother when the family sat on the couch to watch The Jerry Springer Show. When Scott's mother yelled at him, he erupted into a volcano.

"He would beat on her. This was an ongoing thing … probably twice a week on average," Dixie said.

Defiance residents Don and Judy Schaben had long feared that Scott used to pound his dear-old mother. The Schabens lived in their home for more than forty-five years, and they had been acquainted with Scott's mother long before Dixie became a fixture at the home. Scott's mother and stepfather had built the house on Third Avenue.

One morning, Judy Schaben went over to help Bev Feser with painting her house.

"I noticed that Bev was bruised on her legs and her arms, and she was very upset," Judy Schaben said. "And, she said Scott had gotten angry the night before this had happened."

Bev Feser was ashamed and embarrassed. She was certainly not about to let her own husband know that her only child, Scott, had beaten her like a rag doll.

"She had told Al that she fell off the ladder," Judy Schaben recalled.

One time, Scott stormed out of the home after a shouting match with his mother. Scott left and drove over to the county seat of Harlan, where he hung out at a downtown bar.

"About 2 a.m. he called and wanted me to come down and pick him up because the cops was circling around the square," Dixie said. "I ultimately got dressed and came to Harlan, and when I got down to Harlan, I couldn't find him. I finally ended up going back home. When I got home, he was in an argument, and he was hitting his mother, Bev.

"Me and him then got into an argument because I told him to leave her alone. He ultimately picked up a chair and threw it at me across the kitchen. The chair hit the dishwasher."

In some instances, the brown-haired runt took out his misery and grief upon his girlfriend, Dixie. But in those earlier days of their relationship, the abuse was mainly verbal. Those conflicts mostly involved yelling and screaming. But on occasion, Scott slapped and struck Dixie. On other instances, his outrage left her bruised.

Overall, Dixie found his behavior was highly unpredictable.

There were the incidents involving the lawnmower. When the lawnmower would not start, when it was out of gas and Scott had no money, he retreated to his workshop. He sulked. Inevitably, Scott took out his frustration and rage upon Dixie.

"I got beat very bad," Dixie said. "I have had guns pointed at me. He would beat me ultimately. I had a lot of bruises on my face, but most of them was on my arms or my legs so that nobody could see them."

Sometime before Scott's mother passed away in 1994, the elderly and frail woman pulled Dixie aside. She asked for a special favor. It was a favor that Dixie would never forget.

"She asked me to always keep an eye out for him if something ever happened to her."

Chapter 4 — Prince Charming

By late 2000, Dixie Shanahan still remained hopeful that her lunatic of a husband would magically turn into Prince Charming, but that had not happened yet. Dixie ended up with more black eyes. She suffered more purple bruises up and down her arms. She even had a nasty bite mark on her calf.

By this point in their turbulent marriage, Scott had ratcheted up the violence inside their home. During one unforgotten episode, he dragged his wife by her long hair and pulled her down the stairs. There, in the basement, he used a wire hanger to tie her hands behind her back.

He was stark mad. He thought she was about to leave him for Texas.

"You're not going anywhere!" he shouted. "And, you're not taking the kids!"

And so, Scott Shanahan made his wife a prisoner down in her own basement.

"I could let you just sit here and die, and nobody would know the difference," he laughed.

As it turned out, Scott Shanahan left Dixie down in their basement for at least a day. When she had to go the bathroom, she had no choice but to urinate on herself.

Finally, her captor came down the basement stairs, and he set her free. By this time, Dixie was too exhausted and too distraught to call the police to report Scott. She also lost her burning desire to escape from her dangerous and abusive environment of living under Scott's roof.

The basement had turned into a creepy dungeon for poor Dixie Shanahan. One other time, Scott shoved her down the stairs during another feud. "He ultimately threw me down the steps," Dixie said. "It chipped my front teeth."

Fortunately, others who knew or had strong suspicions about the volatile domestic violence felt motivated to intervene on Dixie's behalf. If Dixie was not going to contact the authorities herself, then somebody else needed to do so for her.

On October 6, 2000, Brenda Johnson of Harlan notified the Shelby County Sheriff's Office that Dixie was continuing to endure an abusive home life. This time, however, Dixie was contemplating a clean break. She longed to move to Texas, where she had several relatives, including her sisters. When Brenda showed up at Dixie Shanahan's home to help with the move, nobody came to the door. But, things didn't seem right. Scott and Dixie's vehicles were still parked in their driveway. Johnson's instincts told her that Dixie's abusive husband perhaps had her trapped inside. He was forbidding her from coming to the door.

Johnson tried to open the front door, but it was locked. She went around to the back, but the back door also was locked. Eventually, Johnson called the cops. For the third time since 1997, Shelby County Sheriff's deputies hopped in their patrol cars and made yet another house call to the Shanahan home on Defiance's Third Avenue.

There was a knock on the front door. Startled, Scott Shanahan peeked through the living room curtains, which were drawn closed.

He saw sheriff's deputies converged on his front porch. Scott was livid. He turned into a raging ball of fire.

"Did you call the cops?" he asked Dixie.

"No," she answered truthfully.

Scott marched his wife and his two young children into one of their hallway closets. He forced them into the darkened and confined area. He was the king of his castle and he wasn't about to let the Shelby County Sheriff's Office arrest him for a third crime of domestic violence. He was well aware that the consequences for a third domestic violence conviction would be pretty steep.

"He put us in the closet and stood in front of the door with his foot so that we could not get out," Dixie said.

Shelby County Sheriff's deputies knocked on the door. They rang the doorbell. They got no response. Dixie's friend Brenda Johnson shuddered in fear. Dixie's life might be in grave danger. Or, perhaps Scott had already gone off the deep end. Perhaps Dixie was already dead. Dixie's friend panicked. The thought crossed her mind about grabbing some of the bricks in the front yard and throwing them through the front bay window.

As they walked around the house, Shelby County Chief Deputy Sheriff Mark Hervey realized that most people kept a spare key somewhere around their property. A sharp veteran investigator, Hervey looked around the back patio. Bingo, Hervey noticed an extra key on top of the back porch light. Hervey grabbed the key. He and the other deputies scampered back around to the front of the house. They inserted the key into the front door. The key worked.

As the deputies opened the front door, they announced their presence in a loud and forceful tone. They commanded Scott Shanahan to emerge from the shadows. Moments later, Scott Shanahan popped out of one of the bedrooms along the east edge of the ranch home. Standing behind him was his petrified wife, Dixie. Their two little children huddled with her. Dixie sported two ugly black eyes. One eye was terribly blood shot. There also was a small hole in the hollow core bedroom door where Scott Shanahan had rammed his wife's head.

There was no doubt that Scott Shanahan had beaten his wife, yet again. She told the Shelby County deputies that she had suffered one of her black eyes after Scott had thrown a VCR tape at her face. Her other eye became bloodied and swollen after Scott jabbed her with his fingers days earlier.

Scott Shanahan was hauled away from his home in Defiance in steel handcuffs. Dixie Shanahan went to a nearby hospital. She needed to have her bloody and swollen eyes checked out. At the local hospital, medical doctors realized that a lot of blood had settled around one of Dixie's corneas. Authorities made sure to take several photographs of Dixie's facial lacerations. Such photos could be crucial evidence to use against Scott in court.

For the time being, deadbeat Scott Shanahan was back in the Shelby County Jail, his third such episode for battering his wife.

"He could flip on a nickel," Dixie later said. "He would go out one door, say go out my patio door and be in one frame of mind and come in the other door and be irate."

It seemed as if Scott's third arrest for domestic abuse was the final straw for Dixie Shanahan, age thirty-three at the time. She now had the courage and moral support to make a clean break from Scott Shanahan and escape Defiance for good. With the help and encouragement of her sisters in Sweetwater, Texas, Dixie packed her belongings. She was destined to relocate to Texas, along with her young children. The Lone Star State was quite a long way from Defiance, Iowa, and Scott Shanahan — more than a thousand miles to be exact. But, would the incredible distance be enough to keep Scott Shanahan away?

As Dixie grew accustomed to her new surroundings in Texas, the Shelby County Sheriff's officials back in Harlan, Iowa, still had key legwork to do. But, they did not mind. They were more than eager to proceed with their latest domestic violence case against Scott J. Shanahan. This time, Scott faced real prison time for a change. The Class D felony charges filed by the Shelby County prosecutor, Jeff Larson, signified that Scott Shanahan might very well wind up with five years imprisonment in one of Iowa's rough-and-tough state prison institutions.

Mark Hervey, Shelby County's chief deputy sheriff, was pleased that Dixie had taken proactive steps to free herself from her awful cycle of abuse at the hands of her husband. But, Hervey also had a stern message for her.

"I explained to Dixie that this was a very serious matter now. We were in the felony level and that I needed her as a witness," Hervey said.

Above all, Dixie needed to contact Hervey once she got settled in Texas. Law enforcement in Shelby County, Iowa, needed to know her address and her phone number as court procedures moved ahead against her maniac husband back in Iowa. Hervey also emphasized that Dixie need not worry about any of the traveling costs. The state of Iowa justice system would cover her fares.

A five-year break from Scott Shanahan would have given Dixie an eternity to turn her life around and finally break free of the psychological chains and shackles that were placed upon her by Scott. What's more, a five-year prison term for Scott was more than enough time for Dixie to get a divorce and find a new love, a soul mate, somebody who would treat her with dignity and respect. She was nice and kind. Many of the people around Defiance knew that Dixie deserved better than Scott Shanahan.

"I mean, he was just a loser. He didn't have a job. He didn't work for a living. He didn't draw a paycheck," remarked former longtime Defiance resident Jeff Brightwell.

Brightwell was not alone in his assessment of Scott Shanahan. Many others felt the same.

"He had a heck of a temper. I'd almost call it a mean streak," said Robert Bogler, who had lived around both Harlan and Defiance and was familiar with Scott Shanahan.

* * *

While she lived in Texas, Dixie Shanahan's life was on the rebound. The change of scenery was working. Dixie began to go to counseling. She also enrolled in a nursing school program.

She aspired to become a full-fledged registered nurse.

As the weeks passed, Shelby County Sheriff Chief Deputy Mark Hervey tried his best to convince Dixie that her cooperation with the prosecutor's office was paramount. After all, his agency had devoted lots of time and energy to get to this point against Scott Shanahan. The Defiance man was on the verge of being sent to prison for a Class D felony, domestic abuse assault with injury, plus a charge of false imprisonment, a serious misdemeanor.

Dixie needed to think long and hard about the Shelby County's Sheriff's Office message. She had a monumental decision to make. Back in Iowa, her courtroom testimony would be essential to helping the state of Iowa convict her husband of felony domestic violence. But was she willing to return to Shelby County, Iowa, and walk into a courtroom and testify truthfully against the same wicked man who had treated her like a punching bag over the years? Would she come back to Iowa to testify against the same man who had once yanked her by her long hair across the basement floor and bound her hands with a clothes hanger wire, threatening to keep her locked away in his dungeon of a basement?

"Not only was she the victim, but she would have to be the witness to these charges," Hervey explained.

Even though it seemed that Dixie had made good on her threat to leave her longtime abuser in the dust, she really hadn't.

"He was calling my mom all the time," Dixie said. "He was calling my sisters all the time."

Chapter 5 — Fateful Decision

From the confines of her new temporary home in Texas, Dixie Shanahan sat down and collected her thoughts. On January 15, 2001, she penned the following letter to then-Shelby County Attorney Jeff Larson:

"I am writing this letter to say that I am not wanting to pursue any charges against Scott Shanahan and am asking that the charges be dropped. I will not come back to testify at any time. I will pay all court costs if necessary. I still love my husband and don't want this to happen." Sincerely, Dixie Shanahan

On February 19, 2001, Shelby County Attorney Jeff Larson notified the judge that he was dismissing both criminal charges against twice-previously convicted domestic batterer Scott Shanahan.

Larson was bummed to learn that his key witness, domestic violence victim Dixie Shanahan, was steadfastly refusing to cooperate.

Equally disappointed were members of the Shelby County Sheriff's Office. Dixie's decision was a tremendous letdown.

"We needed her testimony in order to get a felon (sic) conviction, and it was at this time that she explained to me that she had no interest in coming back to Iowa to be a witness," Chief Deputy Sheriff Mark Hervey said.

Scott Shanahan caught a lucky break, though, quite frankly, he had a lot to do with pulling the strings and manipulating his wife into wilting under the pressure.

He got another clean slate. The Shelby County Attorney's Office had missed out on a golden opportunity to brand Scott Shanahan as a convicted felon and send him off to prison for up to five years.

As it turned out, Dixie's stubborn and outright refusal to cooperate with the Shelby County prosecutor's office was only one-half of her fateful and disastrous decision that would come back to haunt her.

After the prosecutor's office had no choice but to dismiss the felony charges against her husband, Dixie Shanahan reconsidered whether staying in Texas was best for her. She contemplated moving back into her home in Defiance, Iowa. And why not? Scott Shanahan was acting like he was ready to become her knight in shining armor, if Dixie just gave him one more chance to turn his life around. Scott was so desperate that he traveled all the way to Texas. He showed up at Dixie's house. He promised to change his ways. This time, he would be a good husband. He even invented a preposterous story, appealing to her sensitive emotions.

"He told me at that point in time that he had hepatitis A. He had been diagnosed with hepatitis A," Dixie said. "That he was going to die."

Of course, Scott Shanahan was not going to die. At least not yet and certainly not from a fake disease that he conjured up as part of his pathetic ploy to woo Dixie and their kids back to his dungeon on Third Avenue in Defiance, Iowa.

By this point, Dixie Shanahan wasn't exactly a naïve teenager. She was nearly thirty-four years old. She had been in a relationship with Scott since she was sixteen. She had endured several years of real-life hard knocks of being married to a first-class loser.

On the flip side, she had plenty of emotional support. Her friends and family were there in her corner. They rooted for her to make a clean break from Scott. Her sisters had insisted that Dixie get rid of Scott Shanahan for good. They wanted nothing to do with her slime ball of a husband.

But, Dixie also knew what she wanted.

"I wanted to keep my family intact," Dixie said. "My major issue was my family."

Scott Shanahan was the missing piece.

And so, around April of 2001, Dixie Shanahan abandoned her pursuit of nursing school and derailed plans of rebuilding her life and raising her two young kids in the state of Texas surrounded by her supportive and loving family. Instead, Dixie decided to reunite with her abusive husband and patch things up. One of her sisters was so stunned and furious to discover that Dixie sneaked out of Texas that she refused to speak with Dixie for more than a year.

Had Dixie stayed in Texas, the odds of successfully rebuilding her life would have been promising. She would have had less reason to be deathly afraid for her own survival. In Texas, Scott Shanahan was no longer the monster who could harm and torment her on a regular basis. But, Dixie's fate was destined for Iowa, not Texas.

Dixie decided to return to the shackles of Scott Shanahan.

Upon returning to Defiance, Dixie and Scott reconciled. And now that Scott's felony domestic abuse case was already dismissed by the prosecutor, this wife-beater no longer fretted about winding up in prison.

In fact, the domestic violence calls involving Scott Shanahan completely stopped.

Two calendar years, 2001 and 2002, came and went without a single law enforcement complaint to the Shelby County Sheriff's Office from domestic-abuse victim Dixie Shanahan.

So, what had happened? Had Scott Shanahan miraculously changed his ways? Had Scott magically turned into Mr. Marvelous, All-American Dad, a peaceful, fun-loving, devoted, and adoring husband? Had Dixie and Scott suddenly become a couple of lovebirds?

Not at all.

Chapter 6 — Where's Scott?

The sad truth of the matter is that Scott and Dixie Shanahan had not reconciled their warped and volatile marriage. Oddly, townspeople continued to encounter Dixie, but not Scott.

By the height of harvest season in 2002, Scott had mysteriously dropped out of sight around Defiance, the little town where he had practically spent his entire life. People who were accustomed to observing Scott spending his afternoons and his evenings hunkered down in his Defiance garage, where he chopped up the tops of his cars and shortened the doors with his useful tools, no longer saw him anywhere. His garage was empty. His tools and his cars languished.

And now, for the very first time, people around the small, tight-knit community were hearing that lifelong resident, Scott Shanahan, age thirty-nine, had apparently decided to pursue greener pastures in another Iowa town, some forty-five minutes away.

Emmett Wise of Defiance vividly remembered the

day that he bumped into Dixie at the Defiance Post Office that October. He asked what Dixie planned to do with one of the tractors that sat outside Scott's garage. "She said that she wanted to sell it," Wise recalled. "She just told me, if I remember right, that Scott was down around Atlantic."

They struck a deal. Wise gave Dixie a check on October 31, 2002. He acquired Scott's old tractor, a Farmall H.

Then, about two weeks later, Wise heard through the small-town grapevine that Scott and Dixie Shanahan were in danger of losing the parcel of property where Scott's garage sat. This time, Wise inquired to Dixie about an older-model Farmall tractor with steel wheels that still occupied the property. Dixie was more than happy to let Wise take Scott's old tractor off her hands.

"She said if I wanted it, to go ahead and take it," Wise remembered.

Talk about a generous move. Dixie gave Wise one of her husband's old tractors for free.

Naturally, Wise figured that Scott Shanahan would eventually pop back into town. Being polite, Wise alerted Dixie that he would just keep Scott's old steel-wheeled tractor outside on his property. That way, when Scott showed his face around Defiance again, he could have his old tractor back.

But, Scott Shanahan's days of showing his face around Defiance were over.

"She told me not to worry about it because Scott wouldn't be back," Wise said.

Turns out, Wise wasn't the only person who was the recipient of Dixie's willingness to get rid of her husband's restored autos. Dixie went so far as to run classified advertisements in the newspapers.

Stephen A. Johnson lived in Council Bluffs, Iowa, the city fifty-five miles south of Defiance, just across the Missouri River from Omaha, Nebraska. Johnson did maintenance work for an apartment company. He and his sons were gear heads. The Johnsons loved to tinker with and restore older model cars. Johnson had a proud collection of several antiques from the late 1930s and 1950s.

In late September 2002, a classified advertisement in the Omaha World-Herald newspaper caught his eye. That advertisement listed several autos for sale. One was a 1937 Chevy. Another was a 1967 Chevelle.

The ad's timing seemed perfect.

Johnson was in the midst of building both kinds of cars. He jumped at the chance to call the phone number listed in the newspaper classified. A woman answered his call. Almost immediately, Johnson recognized that the lady was not an expert on cars like he was. She gave him vague, general descriptions regarding the autos she was trying to sell.

"She had to get them out of a building because apparently the city was repossessing the building," Johnson remembered.

Johnson gleaned from the phone conversation that the woman's husband was shacking up with other ladies and running around partying. She told Johnson that her property was up near Denison.

Initially, Johnson was reluctant. He did not want to become embroiled in a domestic dispute or a city foreclosure related to this woman's piece of property in Defiance. He also knew that Denison was more than an hour's drive from Council Bluffs.

"So I declined on going any further with this ad," Johnson explained.

But a couple of weeks later, a friend convinced Johnson's son to check out the classic cars that were still up for sale.

In any event, Johnson and his son made the long drive to Defiance. That day, they went ahead and purchased the 1967 Chevelle, plus some auto parts from Dixie Shanahan. The total price was eight hundred dollars.

"She handed my son a signed title," Johnson remembered. The title for the Chevelle bore the name of the owner as being Scott Shanahan.

A trail of public records showed that Dixie visited the Shelby County Courthouse on Harlan's downtown square to get a replacement title for Scott's purple-colored 1967 Chevrolet Chevelle Malibu. She officially sold her husband's classic car on October 18, 2002.

* * *

Coinciding with Scott's disappearance, word spread like wildfire around Defiance that Dixie Shanahan was continuing to sell off her vanished husband's prized and precious tools for some cool extra cash. Normally, Scott kept all his tools inside his shop, where he refurbished old cars. The auto garage was about the only thing that Scott Shanahan ever cared about in life. It was where he spent practically all of his time, when he wasn't beating his wife or raising a ruckus inside the couple's home. Now, the hot-tempered, small-town punk was nowhere to be found, even though his Ford truck occupied his driveway on Third Avenue.

People around Defiance began to raise their eyebrows.

Inevitably, Scott Shanahan became the subject of a lot of small-town chit chat and heightened curiosity. Nobody could find him or knew where to look. It was finally during the sweltering summer of 2003, some anonymous resident in town made the decision to dial up the Shelby County Sheriff's Office. And, that's how law enforcement first became aware of his mysterious disappearance. Scott Shanahan was classified as a missing-person case.

Chapter 7 — The Search Begins

Shelby County Sheriff Gene Cavenaugh was a slender, gray-haired man who typically dressed in the uniform.

Cavenaugh had been the sheriff since 1985, after working in the department as a road patrol deputy the previous thirteen years. It was Cavenaugh who got the wheels of justice in motion regarding Scott Shanahan's mysterious vanishing act. The sheriff had received a missing persons report on July 21, 2003.

"I had a call from a concerned citizen that thought maybe we should look into the whereabouts of Scott Shanahan," Cavenaugh explained. "He hadn't been seen for probably a year. This person that called indicated to me that this just wasn't like Scott to just up and leave everything."

Immediately, the sheriff assigned Shelby County Deputy John Kelly to head up to Defiance to speak with Dixie at her house in the hopes of clearing up the problem.

Naturally, Dixie was quite aware of the small-town rumor mill that was festering in Defiance. She even remarked to Deputy Kelly that some people in town were claiming she had buried her husband in their backyard.

The very next day, Sheriff Cavenaugh was confronted by an angry and accusatory Dixie Shanahan inside the sheriff's department.

"Am I being accused of something?" Dixie angrily asked the sheriff.

Cavenaugh responded by saying that Dixie was not being accused of any crime. However, Cavenaugh had a duty to investigate what had happened to Scott.

As the sheriff, Cavenaugh was mostly easy-going and pretty laid-back. But, he was observant and pretty astute. He was a true cop in every sense, unlike some law enforcement professionals who pursued the coveted and highly prestigious office of sheriff for personal gratification or political power. On the contrary, Cavenaugh was genuinely interested in the welfare and well-being of the residents of Shelby County, even if that included people like Scott Shanahan, the bum from Defiance who had three prior arrests for domestic abuse.

With the mystery unresolved, Dixie dished up an uncorroborated tale to the Shelby County Sheriff's Office. She wanted put to rest the nagging questions about her missing husband. She told the sheriff about a man from the small Shelby County community of Irwin named Richard Straw. Apparently, Straw had spotted Dixie's missing husband in the McDonald's restaurant parking lot in Harlan back in April 2003. Dixie urged the sheriff to contact Richard Straw, and he would confirm her story.

Sure enough, Sheriff Cavenaugh got a hold of Richard Straw. In fact, he corroborated Dixie's account. Straw assured the sheriff that he had, in fact, seen Scott Shanahan. Straw even told the sheriff that he distinctly remembered that Scott had on a maintenance uniform at the time.

Indeed, the mystifying case involving the disappearance of the longtime Defiance man was growing stranger and stranger every day.

Many small-town sheriffs might have halted their investigation at that point, but not Shelby County Sheriff Gene Cavenaugh.

On July 24, 2003, the sheriff hopped into his law enforcement vehicle and made the drive back up along Highway 59. When he reached the home of Dixie Shanahan in Defiance, she came outside and met him in her driveway, just like she had done with Sheriff's Deputy Kelly.

This time around, Dixie had a far different story to tell Sheriff Cavenaugh.

She revealed that her husband became violently upset when she revealed that she was pregnant, way back around August of 2002. Scott Shanahan demanded she get an abortion. Dixie defied him. She refused to get an abortion. Scott smacked her. He flew off the handle again. He beat her up once more. But, Dixie did not report the beating to authorities. And that was about it. Scott Shanahan apparently skipped town. He had walked out on his wife and his two young children and set out for a change of scenery. He also must have left on foot because he left behind his only means of transportation — his Ford truck remained back in his driveway.

If Scott Shanahan were enjoying life somewhere other than Defiance, Iowa, Sheriff Cavenaugh wondered what kind of income he might possibly be living on. Dixie suggested that her missing abusive husband had withdrawn all of their bank funds.

Just like Deputy Kelly beforehand, the sheriff of Shelby County also left Dixie Shanahan's driveway without any more clarity. The Shelby County law enforcement agency needed to do more legwork if it was going to unravel the mystery surrounding the missing Defiance man.

Next, the sheriff poked around the small-town post office in Defiance. The postal employees assured Cavenaugh that they did not have any forwarding address for Scott Shanahan's mail. Normally, Dixie just stopped by the post office to pick up any of his mail, the postal employees explained.

Back at his office, Sheriff Cavenaugh entered Scott Shanahan's name into a national law enforcement database for missing and endangered persons. The database was a tremendous gold mine of sorts for police agencies across the country. It cross references the names with those unidentified files of dead persons that appear on a daily basis.

Several days passed. The national missing person's database did not uncover a single record of any person dead or alive from Iowa named Scott Shanahan.

That August, Sheriff Cavenaugh took a much-needed, restful vacation. When he returned to work around August 18, he checked his voice mail messages. One irate caller left the first message. Her name was Dixie Shanahan. She lambasted the sheriff's office and warned the sheriff that his deputy, John Kelly, had better leave her and her kids alone. The second message was not much different. That caller was Jeff Duty, the same guy from Ida Grove who was now carrying on a serious romantic relationship with Dixie Shanahan, even though the whereabouts of her longtime husband, Scott, were unknown across Shelby County. During his phone message to the sheriff, Jeff Duty vowed to hire a lawyer if Sheriff's Deputy John Kelly did not leave him and Dixie's family alone.

In a town of three hundred and fifty people, residents certainly noticed Jeff Duty's constant presence at Dixie and Scott's home during the summer of 2003. Residents were either relieved and happy for Dixie or puzzled and suspicious.

If Dixie was carrying on an adulterous relationship behind Scott's back, where in the world was Scott Shanahan living at these days?

It seemed totally out of character for Dixie to be

engaged in an adulterous relationship while still being tied down in a miserable marriage, with no efforts by either one of them to get a divorce. Furthermore, Scott Shanahan seemed more like the type of jealous hothead who would put a bullet through his wife Dixie's skull if he ever caught her cheating on him with another man, especially a guy who was sleeping with her at his home.

And yet, Scott seemed as invisible as a ghost.

Weekend after weekend, in June, July, August, September, and deep into October of 2003, Jeff Duty regularly parked his vehicle in the driveway near the brown Ford truck that belonged to Scott J. Shanahan.

Duty's constant presence at Scott Shanahan's home was not lost on Sheriff Gene Cavenaugh and his dedicated, hard-working agency trying to unravel the small-town conundrum. Both of the angry voice-mail messages left on the sheriff's answering machine by Dixie and her new steady boyfriend puzzled Cavenaugh. Consequently, the sheriff approached Deputy John Kelly for more background. It turned out that Kelly had happened to be inside the convenience store in Defiance when the store owner noticed one of Dixie's children wander into the store with no shirt or shoes. The owner spoke to the child about the store's policy, and when Kelly overheard the conversation, he chimed in, too. Kelly advised the sheriff that Dixie and her new boyfriend clearly overreacted to the situation.

The missing person investigation pressed onward.

And yet, it seemed like everywhere Sheriff Gene Cavenaugh turned, everywhere the sheriff went, he came upon a colossal dead end.

Cavenaugh grew up in Florida and served four years in the Air Force. From there, he moved to Omaha, Nebraska, and graduated from the University of Nebraska at Omaha campus. He worked as a security officer at the Veterans Affairs hospital in Omaha before moving next door to Iowa to join the Shelby County Sheriff's Office as a deputy sheriff in 1972. The difference between living in metropolitan Omaha and rural Shelby County, Iowa, is night and day. Omaha's sprawling metro consists of about one million people. Shelby County's entire population consists of about thirteen thousand people. Nearly half the county lives around Harlan, which is the county seat. Shelby County typically goes five to ten years, or way longer, in between active murder investigations. In 2003, Sheriff Cavenaugh was not sure he had a murder investigation on his hands, but he was keenly aware that things just didn't seem right in regards to Scott Shanahan.

And so, the curious sheriff investigated.

One by one, Scott Shanahan's longtime neighbors and his few friends all shrugged. Friend Erv Pauley was dumbfounded by Scott's absence. Pauley didn't think Scott would just disappear without staying in contact with him. One of Scott's cousins, Terry Goetz, suspected something bad must have happened. Goetz had not seen Scott since May of 2002. The fact that Dixie was selling off Scott's possessions further deepened Goetz's suspicions.

Scott's longtime neighbors Lavern and Mary Schmitz assured Sheriff Cavenaugh that Scott had been missing for at least a year. The Schmitzes had lived next door to Scott's property for more than thirty years. They had known Scott's parents when they were still alive.

After conducting several interviews with people who knew Scott the best, Sheriff Cavenaugh realized he needed more resources if he had any hope of figuring out what happened to Scott Shanahan. Shelby County's top lawman enlisted the help of a number of additional Iowa law enforcement agencies from across the region. The Cass County Chief Deputy Sheriff Bill Sage was able to verify that Scott Shanahan was absolutely not living in Atlantic, Iowa, the city where Dixie insisted that her husband had relocated. Sage even paid a personal visit to the Atlantic Post Office, where postal employees confirmed that they never had any mailing address information regarding Scott Shanahan ever residing in Atlantic, Iowa.

Sheriff Cavenaugh's own chief deputy sheriff, Mark Hervey, also had a critical role in getting to the bottom of things. Hervey spoke with City of Atlantic Police Chief Roger Muri and explained the disturbing situation. Muri searched through his agency's records. He, too, did not find a single record indicating that any of his Atlantic city police officers ever had any interactions with Scott Shanahan. Muri went so far as to speak individually with all of his uniformed patrol officers. All of them agreed that they never had any contact with the missing man from Defiance, Iowa.

There were a couple of other pivotal places that Shelby County Sheriff Gene Cavenaugh had not checked yet. One was the Iowa job service agency, and the other was the Social Security Administration. The records maintained by the job service agency last showed Scott Shanahan as having a job during the latter part of 2000 — nearly three years prior. The Social Security Administration records mirrored the Iowa job service data.

In summary, there was no indication that Scott Shanahan was working anywhere or drawing unemployed benefits in 2002 or 2003, all the while that he had been missing.

Pondering his next move, Sheriff Gene Cavenaugh decided to run Scott Shanahan's name through a national driver's license database for all fifty states. When the results came back, Scott Shanahan's data only turned up in one state, Iowa. If Scott Shanahan had moved away from Iowa to start a new life, he definitely had not obtained a valid driver's license.

Stuff was now adding up. A disturbing pattern had clearly emerged.

No records existed to show that Scott Shanahan had a job or collected unemployment. Scott never bothered to set up a new mailing address. And, what about the mystery surrounding Scott's vehicle parked in his driveway? How had Scott managed to leave Defiance without a vehicle?

Chapter 8 — The House

By the fall of 2003, Shelby County Sheriff Gene Cavenaugh was at a loss. Practically everywhere the elected sheriff had gone to look for Scott Shanahan, he came up empty. Cavenaugh began to deepen his doubts about Dixie's claim that her husband merely just wandered away and never came back.

"We had known Scott for a number of years, and we knew Scott wasn't the type of individual to up and leave his house and his tools. He was a homebody," Cavenaugh said.

They feared the worst. They presumed that Scott was dead.

By that point, the small-town sheriff's agency utilized additional investigative resources from the Iowa Division of Criminal Investigation. The DCI assigned Special Agent David Jobes as a primary investigator to assist Shelby County with its unusual missing person case.

There were a lot of different scenarios being tossed around. Some investigators thought Dixie buried Scott in the basement. One theory had her breaking up the basement concrete and then re-pouring the cement floor. Authorities also went ahead and searched a vacant farm north of Defiance. The search of the farm property proved fruitless.

During one of their strategy sessions, Shelby County's Chief Deputy Sheriff Mark Hervey, DCI Special Agent David Jobes, and Sheriff Cavenaugh started speculating on where the body of Scott could possibly be.

Hervey offered up his best guess. "I just said, 'in the northeast bedroom.'" Hervey's remark was greeted with funny looks and a couple of chuckles.

"Everybody kind of felt, 'Yeah, sure, sure,'" Hervey added.

About the last place left to look for Scott Shanahan was his own home.

* * *

With all other leads exhausted, Iowa law enforcement officials drew up a sworn affidavit on Friday, October 17, 2003. The formal search warrant application requested the Shelby County Court's permission to search the Shanahan's home at 206 Third Avenue, Defiance, Iowa.

The purpose of the search warrant was to look for Scott's remains.

On October 20, 2003, authorities with the Iowa Division of Criminal Investigation and the Shelby County Sheriff's Office conducted a search of the Shanahan home. That afternoon, authorities made a gruesome discovery in one of the bedrooms. Photo courtesy of The Harlan Newspapers

"His departure seems unlikely, since this was Scott's family home, left to him by his late mother," the court affidavit stated. "There are numerous factors to indicate that Scott Shanahan did not simply leave the Defiance area, but that he likely met some type of foul play."

Western Iowa Judge James Richardson signed the warrant to allow law enforcement officials to enter the private home of Dixie and Scott Shanahan and search their automobiles, property, and outbuildings in the grim hope of finding Scott Shanahan's body. The search warrant was to be carried out on Monday, October 20, 2003. Nobody in law enforcement knew what to expect.

Dixie was oblivious that this was coming.

That Monday morning, Shelby County Sheriff Gene Cavenaugh and DCI Special Agent David Jobes drove up to Defiance. They pulled into Dixie's driveway around 9:30 a.m. When Sheriff Cavenaugh knocked on the door, Dixie answered.

"I asked her if she would be willing to come to Harlan to talk to me about Scott," Cavenaugh recalled.

First, Dixie brought her three young children over to a nearby baby-sitter's place. From there, she drove herself to the Shelby County Sheriff's Office in Harlan. At the time, the cops were guarded and careful not to alert Dixie that her home was going to be searched sometime that day. They preferred to give her one last chance to level with them and be upfront and honest. Inside the sheriff's office, Dixie denied any wrongdoing in connection with her husband's baffling disappearance.

"She again said that he was in Atlantic," Cavenaugh remembered.

Later that morning, Dixie was informed that she needed to leave her 1988 Mercury Grand Marquis at the sheriff's office. The car needed to undergo a forensic examination in the hopes of recovering any blood, DNA, fibers, or trace evidence belonging to Scott.

Ultimately, the sheriff agreed to give Dixie a lift over to a friend's farmhouse out in the country. The property, north of Defiance along Route 59, belonged to Kathryn and Tom Meyers. The drive was mostly quiet. When they reached their destination, Dixie opened the passenger-side door. She looked up and told the sheriff, "Gene, this is where I'll be."

* * *

Kathryn Meyers had known Dixie Shanahan for about a year. The two women became acquainted through baby-sitting. Kathy's grandchildren played with Dixie's kids. Kathy had never met Dixie's husband. She was glad she had not. Kathy had heard horrendous things about Scott Shanahan. Dixie had told Kathy and her husband, Tom, that Scott had walked out on his family and was living somewhere near Avoca, a small western Iowa town off the Interstate 80 corridor.

However, Kathy Meyers knew something was up when, of all people, Shelby County Sheriff Gene Cavenaugh rolled up to the Meyers' property around lunchtime on Monday, October 20, 2003, to drop off Dixie Shanahan.

When Dixie arrived at the farmhouse, she barged into the home, yelling, "Kathy, Kathy."

"She was crying at the time," Kathy Meyers said.

Kathy's husband had just gotten home from work. Dixie wanted some beer and cigarettes.

"She had asked to either borrow the car or if my husband could go get them for her because she needed to calm down," Kathy said.

Tom Meyers agreed to drive down the road to

Brenda's Convenience Store. He fetched an eighteen-pack of canned beer and two packs of cigarettes for Dixie. When he returned, Tom Meyers cracked open an ice-cold can of beer for himself and a can of beer for Dixie. They sat down at the table together. Dixie sipped on her beer and lit up a cigarette.

Whatever was on Dixie's mind was still being bottled up. She wasn't quite ready to talk.

Later that afternoon, the phone rang. Shelby County dispatchers relayed that Dixie's car was done being searched. Dixie could retrieve the car anytime. But investigators were hardly done. Now, they were heading to Defiance to go through Dixie's home.

Kathy Meyers broke the news to Dixie. Dixie grew terrified. Dixie knew that her deepest darkest secret was about to be revealed.

"She said that they would find him," Kathy Meyers said. "She said she couldn't justify whether it was right or wrong, but she just couldn't take it no more."

Dixie's ominous afternoon was about to unfold.

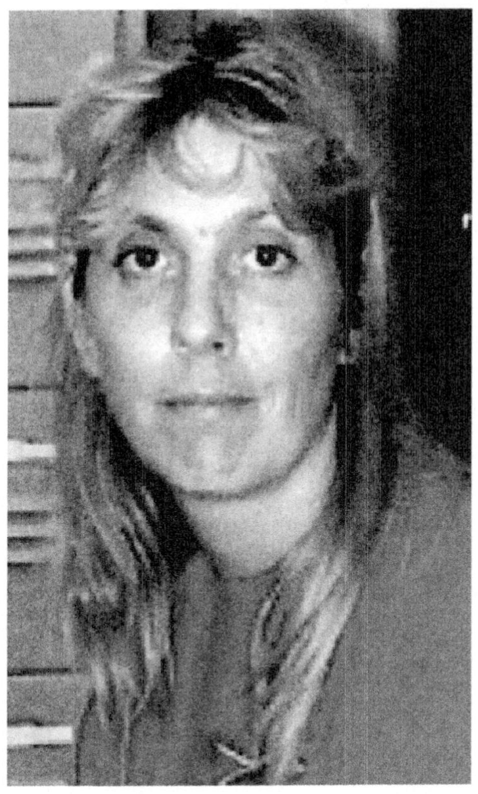

In late October, 2003, Defiance resident Dixie Shanahan, age 36, was taken into custody and charged with the death involving her husband. Photo courtesy of The Harlan Newspapers

* * *

Two Iowa DCI crime lab technicians parked in front of Dixie's garage at the double-wide driveway of her Defiance home. Also on hand was an additional team of experienced, top-level criminal investigators from the DCI's Council Bluffs office. They joined up with Shelby County Chief Deputy Sheriff Mark Hervey to canvass the perimeter of Dixie and Scott's two-acre, tree-lined property.

"We were looking for signs of fresh dirt, something burnt," Hervey said. "It was good having the crime lab there. They didn't want everybody stomping through the house."

After taking several exterior photos of the ranch, DCI crime lab technicians Paul Bush and Karl Franzenburg entered the home. Inside, they drew up an interior sketch of the ranch dwelling. Their drawing entailed floor plans, dimensions, and the various rooms and hallways. The back of the house featured a dining room, kitchen, and laundry area. There was a bathroom tucked in the back, plus another living room that looked like it was serving as a spare bedroom.

The main living room was toward the front. A long, narrow hallway was off to the right of the front door. The first room down the hallway was a children's bedroom. That room contained a set of bunk beds, a closet, and a children's clothes dresser. The main bathroom within the home was along that hallway. It contained a toilet, shower, and bathtub. It also had a second door that led into the master bedroom.

That afternoon, Iowa DCI criminologist Paul Bush tried to open the door.

"But, it was blocked," Bush said. "There was

something behind that door so you couldn't open it."

Chapter 9 — The Discovery

The long, dark hallway that led to Dixie and Scott Shanahan's master bedroom was filled with lots of clutter. There were children's toys, folding chairs, cardboard boxes, a vacuum cleaner, a picnic cooler, and other junk.

The litany of objects made it extremely challenging for law enforcement officials to navigate their way safely down the hallway without tripping over themselves.

Once he converged upon the door, criminologist Paul Bush spotted a bathroom towel rolled underneath the wooden bedroom door. And, there was more. Down on the carpet was an unlit scented candle inside a jelly jar. A small portable air freshener also was on the carpet beside the bathroom towel.

"What we did at this point then was to remove the towel from the doorway and attempt to enter that master bedroom," Bush said.

Once all the objects, including the large cardboard television and VCR boxes, were finally removed from blocking the door, Bush and his partner tried to open that mysterious master bedroom door.

"This door was locked," Bush said.

Fortunately, Iowa DCI Special Agent David Jobes was around on the property. Jobes had a small pen knife to pry the door lock open.

When the door was pried open, the investigators were aghast.

"First thing that we noted when we opened the doorway was a bad odor in the room," Bush said.

The stink was hideous.

The smells were so rancid that those Iowa law enforcement officials who were there that late October weekday afternoon would never, ever, forget the stench.

Actually, the inside of the bedroom consisted of a pair of nightstands on each side of the bed. There was a night lamp. There was a bed in the middle of the room.

And there was something else.

"There was a large lump in the bed," Bush said.

Without a doubt, there was something odd and creepy about that bed.

Slowly, Bush approached the east side of the bed. He and the others needed to find out, once and for all, whether that large lump buried underneath the white-colored blankets and covers was the missing body of Scott Shanahan.

Bush peered under the covers for a quick gaze.

What he saw was downright mortifying and gross. Then he stepped back.

"There were lots of insects, dead insect larvae, and eggshell casings there, and I just looked slightly under that white blanket," Bush said.

A comforter and bedspread helped conceal the body in the middle of the bed. A white blanket was draped over the entire body. When the top of the blankets were pulled back, the person's head and shoulder area were exposed.

Bush pulled back the bed sheets and covers to explore further.

"Once I noted that it appeared there was a body under that top white blanket, we then notified the county medical examiner and waited for him to arrive before we touched or moved anything else," Bush said.

* * *

Shelby County Sheriff Gene Cavenaugh's cellular phone rang while he was out in the county conducting interviews. He took the call. Then, he drove straight to Defiance.

The criminologists escorted the sheriff through the home.

"Once we entered in the house, there was a real foul odor emitting from the residence," Cavenaugh said. "We went back to the hallway to the right, off of the living room, to a northeast bedroom, and there in that bedroom, there was some human remains on the bed."

Cavenaugh actually did not expect to find Scott Shanahan's body inside the house on that memorable day in Shelby County law enforcement history.

"To our surprise, he was still in the house," Cavenaugh said. "If it had been me, I would have tried to get rid of the body. We went into this with the feeling the body is gone. But it was there, to our surprise."

Mark Hervey, the chief deputy sheriff for Shelby County at that time, still remembers being alerted to the state crime lab's find in the northeast bedroom. The smell was plain awful. And Hervey will never forget the sight of countless blow flies present upon the body.

"It had somewhat mummified itself," Hervey said of the body.

After the medical examiner arrived, Bush stuck around the bedroom. He carefully and properly documented what was clearly a death scene like no other.

Indeed, lots of tiny insects had munched on the body

that had been hidden underneath the covers for a rather extended length of time. Someone who looked at Bush's crime-scene photos might mistake the dead insect casings for blood stains or droplets. These were definitely not blood stains, Bush determined.

"All these little dark dots … along the fitted sheet are actual casings of larvae or pupae of insects," Bush said.

The dead man's head rested on a pillow. One of his arms rested against another pillow. It looked plainly like he died in his sleep. He was laying on his right side.

"He's clothed only in a pair of white briefs," Bush noted. "Between his legs is a pillow, and then right at the end of his left foot there is a remote control, like a TV remote."

That afternoon, Bush also made a startling discovery. His important find set the wheels of justice into motion.

A piece of plastic was found inside the back of the dead man's scalp.

"We noted a hole in the back side of the head," Bush said.

The body in the bed was so badly decayed that authorities simply could not say for certain that the remains were Scott Shanahan, but who else could they be?

* * *

A few miles up the road, at 3:25 p.m., fear, panic, and paranoia set in at the Iowa farmhouse north of Defiance.

When Dixie Shanahan glanced out the window, she knew exactly why the two special visitors brandishing shiny badges had just pulled into the driveway of Tom and Kathy Meyers. Dixie retreated. She hid in the bedroom closet. She was doomed.

Sheriff Gene Cavenaugh and his investigative helper, DCI Special Agent David Jobes, exited their squad car and went up to the Meyers' door.

They were there for Dixie.

"First of all," Kathy Meyers recalled, "she had said that she wanted us to tell them that she wasn't there, and we told her that we couldn't do that."

Finally, Dixie emerged from her hiding spot.

"Is she under arrest?" Kathy Meyers meekly asked.

"And before Agent Jobes and I could say yes, Dixie replied, 'Yes I am,'" Cavenaugh vividly remembered.

Chapter 10 — The Autopsy

At around 4:30 p.m., the Pauley Jones Funeral Home in Harlan had the morbid task of hauling away what was left of the body found in Defiance at 206 Third Avenue.

Removing the human remains was an adventure because of the advanced state of decomposition.

"Anything that the body was lying on, the fitted sheet and the mattress pad, we just kind of rolled up together and placed in the body bag to be transported along with the body to Des Moines for autopsy," Bush said.

After the body was delicately taken out of the bed, Bush moved in closer. He inspected the mattress, since it still was not abundantly clear what caused this person to die. There were no bullet holes in the mattress.

"The mattress was intact except for the fact that it had a lot of biological or body stain fluids that were on it," Bush said.

There was, however, an eerie distinct impression of the dead body etched into the bed mattress. This made sense, given the advanced state of decomposition.

"The fluids or liquid portion basically seeps out of the body and, again, is absorbed into whatever the body is lying on, and in this case, it was the mattress," Bush noted.

Before calling it a most unusual day, Bush made a careful visual inspection of the master bedroom. He panned the walls. He studied the ceiling. He checked the carpet. He hoped to find bullet fragments and signs of bloodstains.

But he did not have any such luck.

However, an arm's length from the bed, the top drawer of the nightstand contained a couple of plates of marijuana. There were several little plastic baggies with small amounts of marijuana in them.

Naturally, authorities presumed the body in the bed belonged to Scott Shanahan, the same Iowa man who had vanished from Defiance fourteen months prior. But, was it really him?

* * *

The human remains removed from the Defiance home were delicately delivered to the Broadlawns Medical Center in Des Moines for an autopsy. The DCI's Paul Bush was present, along with his fellow

DCI crime lab partner, Karl Franzenburg.

Dr. Julia Goodin led the autopsy, and she was joined by her capable medical assistants, Paul Steinback and Jackie Short.

Dr. Goodin had about fourteen years of experience as a professional forensic pathologist. She graduated from medical school at the University of Kentucky. She had done her residencies at the Vanderbilt University Medical Center in Nashville, Tennessee. She did her forensic pathology fellowship in Baltimore, Maryland. She was the state of Iowa's chief medical examiner at the time the body bag of human remains was brought to her building on Tuesday, October 21, 2003. She had examined her share of dead bodies, but what was left of this corpse was morbid and downright disgusting.

This adult male's body was reduced to the size of a kindergartener.

"The body only weighed forty-one pounds at that point," Dr. Goodin testified. "The head was somewhat deformed due to fractures of the skull, and there was clearly a shotgun wound to the back of the head."

The decay was quite evident to those attending the autopsy procedure.

"The body was markedly decomposed, partially skeletonized, and partially mummified," Dr. Goodin later testified. "There was a golden brown stringy stuff that had been left by insects covering much of the body. The body was only clad in a pair of undershorts, and it was laying on a sheet and some pillows."

Shotgun pellets and plastic wadding from a shotgun shell cap were recovered from the dead man's skull. Chemical tests identified the presence of Tylenol and aspirin in the man's body. No other drugs were found in the body.

However, the skull exhibited no exit wounds.

"Most of the pellets remained in the head," Dr. Goodin observed. "I listed the cause of death on the autopsy report as a shotgun wound to the back of the head and the manner of death as homicide."

Some skin was collected from the body. This helped obtain fingerprints from the body in the hopes of making a positive identification, Bush noted.

There was now no doubt that the body belonged to Scott Shanahan.

Chapter 11 — Dixie's Arrest

On the same day as the autopsy, Dixie Shanahan started becoming accustomed to wearing a standard-issue, orange-colored jail jumpsuit.

Dixie Shanahan is escorted away from the Shelby CountyCourthouse in handcuffs by Sheriff Gene Cavenaugh shortly after a juryreached a unanimous verdict in her murder trial. Photo courtesy of The Des Moines Register

Dixie's arrest on first-degree murder charges jolted the little town of Defiance, Iowa. Everybody had an opinion about whether Dixie was justified to slay her abusive husband.

"I think everybody in town knew something was going to happen to one or the other," neighbor Don Schaben remarked to the Omaha World-Herald newspaper.

At the time of her arrest, Dixie had three young children, including an eight-month-old infant. All three kids would grow up without knowing their father. And, many people in town believed that was for the best.

"Everybody knows she had hell on Earth until she could take it no more," Charlie Goetzinger, a bartender at Tobe's tavern in Defiance, told the newspaper.

Customers who bellied up to the bar at Tobe's watering hole tried to tip the scales of justice in Dixie's favor.

The small-town western Iowa bar displayed a large canister inside the business to raise proceeds to bail Dixie out of jail before her case proceeded to trial. The sign on the jar read, "Free Dixie: Lawyer Fees. Show your support."

This canister at one of the taverns in Defiance, Iowa, encouraged patrons to donate cash to bail Dixie Shanahan out of jail after she was formally charged with killing her husband. Photo courtesy of The Des Moines Register

A judge set her bail at one hundred and fifty thousand dollars. The Council Bluffs office of the Iowa Public Defender's Office was appointed as her legal defense counsel. Within a short period of time, the town and Dixie's supporters quickly came up with the required fifteen thousand dollars in cash, or ten percent, to bail Dixie out of jail as she awaited trial.

At the time of her arrest, Dixie Shanahan was thirty-six years old, though she looked older. Perhaps her rough life, exhaustion, and being smacked around all the time led to premature aging.

Based on town sentiment, most people considered Scott Shanahan a good-for-nothing loser. If the town's biggest deadbeat ended up with a shotgun blast through the back of his skull at the hands of his abused and tortured wife, Dixie, all for the better, many people thought.

Brightwell, the former Defiance resident, remembered the time when Scott Shanahan grew infuriated upon learning that Dixie had become pregnant.

"Now she won't be able to work and bring in a paycheck," Scott remarked. "What do I do now?"

Brightwell told Scott to sell off one of his many antique autos. The suggestion fell on deaf ears.

Cindy LaDuke remembered the time when Scott Shanahan stormed into a downtown Defiance storefront as if he were a Tasmanian devil.

That day, he was incensed that the city clerk had sent him a notice that his utilities were being temporarily disconnected. Scott had not been paying his monthly water bills for quite some time.

"When he came in, he was shaking all over," LaDuke recalled. "His fists were clenched, and his teeth were clenched. And, he was talking to me through clenched teeth, very angry."

The murder case against Dixie Shanahan sparked an enormous outcry across the country, largely from various domestic violence groups and organizations. In turn, various national news media organizations latched onto the baffling small-town murder case, including the Los Angeles Times. On December 26, 2003, the LA Times published a story with a

Defiance, Iowa, dateline headlined, "Townsfolk Look the Other Way in Abuse and Slaying."

The article, approximately thirty-five paragraphs in length, was largely sympathetic to Dixie's plight as a murder defendant.

"Iowa juries in the past have proved sympathetic to battered women. In the most notorious case, in 1992, a jury acquitted Betty Friedberg of murdering her husband after the defense presented evidence that he had kicked, shocked, choked and threatened her in more than a year of abuse."

Dixie's public defender, Greg Steensland, was quoted extensively throughout the national newspaper story. That article also included a couple of anonymous comments from purported residents of Defiance, who were interviewed by the writer.

* * *

Regardless of how Iowans felt about Scott Shanahan, folks bristled at the thought of Dixie Shanahan sharing her home with her dead husband's corpse.

And, Dixie didn't just occupy the home with what was left of Scott for a matter of just days, weeks, or months, but well over a year. Astonishingly, she continued to stay there with her three young children, including her newborn.

She just acted as if her kids' dear-old dad had run off and deserted the family.

Every night, as Dixie sat down at the kitchen table for home-cooked meals, or gave her children baths, or sat on the living room couch to watch television, Scott Shanahan's dead body was decomposing just down the hallway. The always-closed bedroom door kept the putrid smell from percolating throughout the rest of Dixie's house. The rolled up bathroom towels, the sweet scented candles, and air-fresheners also worked really well.

"She had told her kids not to go in there," Sheriff Cavenaugh said.

It was even more stunning to learn after the fact that Dixie had invited guests in her home all the while, including her four-year-old daughter's preschool Head Start program assistant teacher, among others.

Defiance resident Marc Carl also had been inside the Shanahan home while Scott's corpse was under the pulled-up blankets in the back bedroom. He, too, was oblivious to the floor towels, scented candles, and air fresheners and various objects that were propped up against the bedroom door.

"I never even noticed any candles," Marc Carl told the court. "The only time I went close is to use the restroom, come back, and we was out on the patio."

Marc Carl and his wife, Marcie, had become close friends with Dixie. The Carls considered Scott Shanahan vicious and evil. They both testified that they had no knowledge of Scott's untimely demise.

Marcie Carl acted dumbfounded by the Shelby County

Sheriff's Office's late October 2003 discovery of Scott's remains within the home's master bedroom.

"I didn't know he died," Marcie Carl later testified.

* * *

Another Iowan who didn't know anything about the body in the bedroom was Jeff Duty. He lived about forty miles from Defiance in the town of Ida Grove. He happened to be at Marc and Marcie Carl's property for an intimate Memorial Day weekend barbeque in 2003.

Dixie stopped over at the barbeque, and Cupid's arrows soon struck Jeff and Dixie. Duty was forty-two, Dixie was almost thirty-six. Almost overnight, the two grown adults turned into lovebirds. Unbeknownst to Jeff Duty, Marc and Marcie Carl, and the other Memorial Day party guests, Dixie's husband Scott had already been dead the previous nine months.

With a new man in her life, Dixie became a changed woman. Jeff Duty swept her off her feet. He spent most of his free time in Dixie's companionship. Unlike Dixie's deadbeat husband, her new man had worked a steady job over the past ten years at a large manufacturing company in Ida Grove. Duty and Dixie even went on a vacation together.

Obviously, a lot of people were curious about Dixie's new Romeo, this new guy hanging around town named Jeff Duty. In the wake of the discovery of Dixie's dead husband, the new boyfriend also became the center of intrigue and everybody's morbid curiosity. How in the world had Jeff Duty stayed overnight at Dixie's home for all of those months and been completely oblivious to the fact that Scott Shanahan's remains were hidden behind the always-shut master bedroom door?

Bear in mind that Jeff Duty had full roam of Dixie's house during those many nights he stayed there. He became accustomed to the fact that the always-shut master bedroom door was cluttered with children's toys, gigantic television boxes, folded chairs, and a party cooler.

However, the Ida Grove man steered clear of the far northeast corner of the home, where the master bedroom was located.

"I never went back there," Duty later testified.

When Jeff Duty stayed at Dixie's home in 2003 after Scott had already been fatally shot with a shotgun, he and Dixie slept in what was known as the living room bedroom, over behind the kitchen toward the back of the house. Dixie's two oldest children typically slept on the couches in the front living room. They liked to watch television as they drifted off to sleep. Shelby County Sheriff Cavenaugh was always puzzled by Jeff Duty's lack of curiosity.

"There was no evidence that he was involved in any of this," Cavenaugh said. "But, I think with most people, I think their curiosity would have gotten the better of them. What's in this room that always happens to be kept shut?"

Since Duty knew the master bedroom door was always closed, he just acted as if the far northeast bedroom at 206 Third Avenue was off-limits to him.

"I just thought a bunch of abuse must have happened back there and (Dixie) just didn't want to stay back there anymore," Duty said.

On one instance, Duty questioned Dixie about a weird smell lingering in the house, but that was the one and only time. In that instance, the air conditioner unit just kicked on.

"I smelled like a musty smell, but that was just for a couple of minutes," Duty remembered. "She said she needed a dehumidifier."

Dixie needed more than a dehumidifier. She could have used a hazmat team.

Chapter 12 — Money Trouble

After the Shelby County Sheriff's Office began probing Scott Shanahan's disappearance during the hot and humid summer of 2003, a wise decision was made to scrutinize the couple's finances.

The court subpoena crafted by Sheriff Gene Cavenaugh and Iowa Division of Criminal Investigation Special Agent David Jobes turned up more unsettling information — the circumstances surrounding Scott's demise and the logical impetus for his murder.

When Scott Shanahan's dear-old mother, Beverly Feser, died in 1994, she left him a nice fortune of at least one hundred and forty-four thousand dollars, plus the ranch house nestled on the two-acre, tree-lined lot in the town of Defiance. The one hundred and forty-four thousand-dollar mutual fund investment account was with Prudential.

In short order, the mutual fund did rather well. It grew to a value of one hundred and seventy-seven thousand dollars within a few years.

However, from 1998 to 2002, Dixie and Scott Shanahan began to live dangerously and rather foolishly with their newfound wealth. They used the mutual fund as a non-stop checking account. They used that money to pay off all their bills and cover living expenses. By August of 2002, the Prudential fund that once had a nice tidy sum of one hundred and seventy-seven thousand dollars had fallen to only eighty dollars.

"It basically went to nothing," Prudential investment representative Phillip Elder later testified.

He had grown alarmed by the ominous signs taking place with the once-flush mutual fund. In 2002, Elder called the Shanahan home. He asked for Scott. Dixie answered. She told him that her husband wasn't around.

"Be careful," Elder warned her. "There's not any money left in this account."

"I'll pass it along," she nonchalantly responded.

Truth be known, since neither Dixie, nor Scott had a job, they had been drawing down on their Prudential mutual fund by at least three thousand to four thousand dollars every month.

Dixie and Scott were in serious, bleak dire straits financially. Their marriage remained on the rocks. A third child was on the way. They also still had to pay about five hundred and seventy-five dollars per month on their mortgage. Now, they were on the verge of losing their home, and Scott was in danger of losing his lot across the street, where his garage was filled with tools and old cars.

By September of 2002, the once-flush mutual fund account was being overdrawn. And yet, that did not stop Dixie Shanahan from continuing to write out even more bad checks. Dixie kept on writing more checks because, after all, she had a third child on the way.

Authorities discovered that Dixie had written at least five bad checks at the Wal-Mart retail store in Denison. Her Wal-Mart retail purchases included women's clothing and baby items. Those checks were signed by Scott J. Shanahan, though there was no way that Scott J. Shanahan had purchased those items because he was very clearly dead by that time and starting to stink up the master bedroom of his house.

A law enforcement subpoena for access to Scott Shanahan's bank records later showed that his bank account had been overdrawn on multiple instances during the summer of 2002 — while Scott was still alive. However, subsequent bank records throughout the summer of 2003 showed that Scott's bank account had been dormant for about a year. Scott had banked for years in the nearby little town of Earling.

As for the home mortgage, Scott Shanahan was listed as the executor. And, this made perfect sense, since Scott inherited the home on Third Avenue after his mother died in 1994. Although Scott and Dixie had lived there together for more than a decade, the two didn't get married until the following year, 1995.

On October 16, 2002, the bank handling Scott's home mortgage received a letter purportedly written by Scott J. Shanahan.

"This is to notify you that I would like my wifes (sic) name added to this account with mine due to the fact that she is handling the bills and needs to be in contact with you concerning the loan and I (sic) unable to do so. This will allow her to contact you regarding this loan." Signed Scott J. Shanahan

For sure, Scott had not written that letter. His decomposing body had been covered over by blankets in his master bedroom for at least six weeks by that point.

During the fall of 2002, Dixie went ahead and filed an application with the Iowa Department of Human Services. She indicated that she was down to fifty dollars in cash and about five hundred and fifty dollars in a checking account. She noted in her application that she was separated from her husband, and he might be living in Atlantic.

The Iowa DHS approved her public welfare application. This signified that in addition to having lied about her dead husband's whereabouts, she now was collecting a monthly stipend of four hundred and twenty-six dollars from the Iowa taxpayers. In March of 2003, Dixie's monthly public welfare stipend was increased to four hundred and ninety-five dollars after the birth of Dixie and Scott's third child, Brittany.

"The money from that inheritance ran out, as I recall, in June or July (of 2002). Dixie Shanahan killed Scott about a month or so later. It looked to me that she was willing to put up with the violence as long as the money was there. Once it was gone, she decided to get rid of him," prosecutor Charles Thoman said.

Chapter 13 — The Prosecutor

Back in 2003, Charles Thoman was assigned to the Area Prosecutions Division of the Iowa Attorney General's Office. Thoman was a familiar face in many of the small-town courthouses. He often was called upon to handle or assist with the prosecution in such delicate and rare high-profile murder cases where the local elected prosecutor was woefully inexperienced or had a real or perceived conflict of interest.

Thoman's chief geographic territory was western Iowa. He was not assigned to prosecute crimes in specific counties, but rather, he handled a general region of territory.

Shelby County, Iowa, where the homicide of Scott Shanahan had taken place, was halfway between Thoman's base office in Sioux City and the home office of the Iowa Attorney General's staff located in the state capital of Des Moines.

Charles Thoman of Sioux City was an experienced Assistant Iowa Attorney General who drew the assignment to handle the prosecution of Dixie Shanahan.

Thoman first became aware of the Shanahan case after receiving a phone call from Shelby County Attorney Marcus Gross Jr. At that point, Thoman admittedly was quite unfamiliar with the circumstances involving the Dixie Shanahan case.

"When Marcus Gross called on the Shanahan case, I was feeling somewhat burned out from the Boss prosecution," Thoman recalled. "I told Marcus I would call Des Moines and have them assign an area prosecutor from Des Moines."

Thoman had just concluded in Le Mars, Iowa, an enormously high-profile small-town murder case that had shaken Plymouth County. There, Donald

Boss Jr. and his wife, Lisa, had resided in the small town of Remsen. The couple had several children, plus several adopted foster kids.

The Sioux City Journal newspaper chronicled the grisly tragedy involving the deplorable murder of ten-year-old Timothy Boss. According to the newspaper, Michigan relatives of foster child Timothy Boss had contacted authorities in Iowa around January of 2002 because nobody had seen or heard from Timothy Boss for a long period of time. In late February 2002, a gruesome discovery was made. The boy's remains were discovered underneath the basement floor of his foster parents' home in Remsen, Iowa. According to court testimony, ten-year-old Timothy was killed February 23, 2000, after being strapped to a metal chair and beaten.

As a result of a plea agreement with prosecutors, Lisa Boss was given a fifty-year prison sentence. However, Donald Boss Jr., the foster father, was convicted by a jury of first-degree murder. A judge in Plymouth County sentenced Donald Boss Jr. to life in prison without parole.

When Thoman conferred with his colleagues in the AG's Office in Des Moines about the Shanahan case, his supervisors nixed the idea of assigning a different prosecutor to assist the small-town Shelby County Attorney's Office. Instead, the bosses pegged Thoman to assist with the prosecution.

Unbeknownst to Thoman, he would do a lot more than assist.

In smaller communities, it's not unusual for conflicts of interest to arise involving the lawyers because most everybody knows everybody. And, that's what happened in the case of State of Iowa v. Dixie Lynn Shanahan.

Shelby County Attorney Marcus Gross Jr. of Harlan had previously served as the criminal defense lawyer for Scott Shanahan during one of Scott's domestic violence cases.

As a result, Gross pretty much had no involvement in the ensuing courtroom murder case proceedings that moved forward in the county seat of Harlan against Dixie.

"Shortly after that, when it became known that Marcus Gross had a potential conflict of interest, my assignment evolved from assisting the county attorney into becoming sole prosecutor," Thoman explained.

For Thoman, a gray-haired assistant prosecutor in his early fifties, having the assignment of ensuring justice for Scott Shanahan was an odd and peculiar predicament. Most everybody around Defiance hated Scott Shanahan or bore a strong disliking toward the man. They considered him the town's rat. Most people despised him.

Therefore, Thoman's pursuit of a murder conviction against Dixie Shanahan was quite a contrast with most of the murder cases he had handled for the Iowa Attorney General's Office. Murder victim Scott Shanahan's violent behavior toward his wife had a major impact on the case.

"Defendant Dixie Shanahan was viewed as a victim of domestic violence, which was certainly true," Thoman said, "and this created a great deal of sympathy for her throughout Shelby County. Local, state, and national domestic violence groups also supported the defendant. I received calls from angry activists from Florida and elsewhere demanding to know why I was prosecuting this woman. Of course, the public did not have access to the investigative files and evidence that I had, which revealed in my mind a significant element."

* **

The first major legal battle for the prosecution occurred on January 20, 2004, in the Shelby County Courthouse in downtown Harlan.

Iowa Fourth District Judge Charles L. Smith III out of Council Bluffs was assigned to preside over the noteworthy evidentiary hearing.

Because Dixie had blown all her and Scott's money, she was flat broke when she was arrested. As a result, the court assigned her to be represented by Council Bluffs Public Defender Greg Steensland. Steensland was a lanky, silver-haired public defender with a mustache and glasses.

On Dixie's behalf, he took issue with the search warrant affidavit.

Dixie's lawyer argued that the Shelby County

Sheriff's Office had lacked sufficient legal probable cause to invade her home back on October 20, 2003. Therefore, the discovery of Scott Shanahan's mummified remains amounted to an illegal search of Dixie's property, based on his legal purview.

"In this case we have a quote, 'Concerned person' unnamed and no information resulting from that person that would lead to any kind of an ultimate determination of probable cause," Steensland argued to Judge Smith. "In this case, we have no request for consent. No refusal for consent."

Steensland was a scrappy defense lawyer and a fairly shrewd legal strategist.

He also pointed out that at least one person had claimed to see Scott Shanahan as late as April of 2003 in a Harlan, Iowa, McDonald's restaurant parking lot.

"Basically, your honor, I don't want to belabor the argument here," Steensland declared in court. "You're going to have to sit down and make your comparison, look at the affidavit and determine if probable cause exists. We do not believe it does exist in this case for the reasons I have stated. Thank you."

If Judge Smith ruled in favor of the defendant and rejected the Shelby County Sheriff's Office search warrant, the prosecution's case was pretty much skunked. The murder case probably would have been dismissed. Dixie Shanahan would have been able to return home and not have to worry about first-degree murder charges dangling over her head the rest of her life.

That day in court, Thoman, the assistant attorney general from Sioux City, spoke for the prosecution. He saw the case starkly different, though he was careful not to reveal his entire deck of cards against Dixie Shanahan, at least not for now anyway.

First, he patted the Shelby County Sheriff's Office on the back for being diligent and relentless in its pursuit of the truth.

"They searched out friends and acquaintances of Scott Shanahan, and they're specifically named in the affidavit," Thoman advised the court. "And, these friends, they all advised the sheriff that, yeah, I haven't seen Scott for at least a year. And, one of them even went so far as to say if he was going to leave Defiance, Shelby County, he would have told me."

In the case at hand, Thoman advised Judge Smith that Dixie's own words cast deep and serious suspicion upon herself in Scott's suspected death at that time. He reminded the judge of some of Dixie's cryptic and quite defensive statements.

"'Why are you concerned? Are you trying to say I've done something wrong?'" Thoman recited. "She fabricated stories about where she was, gives inconsistent stories about where he was. When the sheriff comes out to meet her the next day, rather than let him come up to the door of her home, she runs out and meets the sheriff at his squad car in the driveway."

In fact, Dixie's defense lawyer was grasping at straws by pointing out that a man named Richard Straw had supposedly spotted Scott Shanahan at a Harlan McDonald's in April of 2003.

"Well, of course, in hindsight, we know that's wrong," Thoman told the judge. "That's just not the case. He couldn't have seen him. But the information he gave to the sheriff's office and the (Division of Criminal Investigation) and the police that is in the affidavit was that he, Mr. Straw, saw Scott Shanahan wearing a uniform, indicating that he was employed."

Instead, the Shelby County Sheriff's Office dug deeper and came across irrefutable, conclusive, rock-solid proof through the Iowa job service and federal Social Security Administration that Scott Shanahan was not collecting any unemployment or drawing a wage since he turned up missing in Defiance in August of 2002.

Homicide victim Scott Shanahan was fatally shot in the head by his wife Dixie with one of his own shotguns. Jurors had to determine whether Scott's wife had killed him during an act of

self-defense or whether his death was a vicious act of murder.
Photo courtesy of The Des Moines Register

"Really, what it boils down to, your honor, is it reasonable to believe that something bad may have happened to Scott Shanahan?" Thoman asked the judge. "This information as set forth in the affidavit essentially discredits Mr. Straw's statement saying that he thought he'd saw Scott here in Harlan about last April."

The ultimate question put before Judge Smith was whether the Shelby County Sheriff's Office had reasonable suspicion to infer that Scott Shanahan met foul play on his property.

"The State has shown probable cause, and we'd ask the court to overrule the motion to suppress," Thoman urged.

That afternoon, Judge Smith took the oral arguments from both sides under advisement. The judge carefully weighed both viewpoints. But in the end, Judge Smith's ruling was hardly a shocker.

Dixie Lynn Shanahan's first-degree murder case was assigned criminal docket number FECR 06475. Her criminal case would proceed to a jury trial in Shelby County.

Chapter 14 — Dixie's Gamble

It's quite common for prosecutors and defense lawyers to strike deals to avert jury trials. About three weeks before the date of Dixie's jury trial, Judge Charles Smith III arranged for an informal pre-trial meeting with the lawyers working on this extraordinary high-profile murder case.

Thoman recalled that Judge Smith asked what kind of plea bargain had been extended to Dixie.

"I told him I had made no offer," Thoman said. "The judge was adamant that I consider making a plea offer to the defendant."

During the discussions, Dixie's lead defense attorney, Greg Steensland, revealed that Dixie would plead guilty to the felony crime of voluntary manslaughter if offered the opportunity.

The historic Shelby County Courthouse, located in the center of the downtown city square in Harlan, Iowa, was the setting in April 2004 for the high-profile murder trial of State versus Dixie Lynn Shanahan. Photo courtesy of The Harlan Newspapers

"I had never encountered such a situation before, nor have I since," Thoman explained. "It was apparent that the judge felt this case should be resolved by plea agreement."

There was a monumental difference in the potential prison sentences.

If Dixie took the voluntary manslaughter plea deal, she would be sentenced to serve ten years in prison, but, theoretically, she could be released from the penitentiary after serving as little as two-and-a-half years in Iowa's prison system. On the other hand, a first-degree murder conviction in Iowa carried a punishment of life in prison with no parole.

After the unorthodox meeting in Council Bluffs, Iowa, prosecutor Thoman made the hour-long drive up to the Shelby County seat of Harlan. There, at the sheriff's office, he huddled with Sheriff Cavenaugh and Chief Deputy Sheriff Mark Hervey. The two law enforcement leaders sensed that Dixie had widespread community support on her side. Her slain husband was viewed in a negative light. Resolving Scott Shanahan's homicide with a plea agreement seemed appropriate to them, according to Thoman.

Later on, Thoman spoke with one of the officials at the Iowa Division of Criminal Investigation to make him aware of the possible plea agreement.

"While neither of us were particularly satisfied that voluntary manslaughter should be offered, in light of everything, especially the views of the sheriff and chief deputy who were attuned to the community's feelings, I made the final call to make that plea offer," Thoman said.

And so, the consensus was reached. Dixie would be offered a chance to plead guilty to voluntary manslaughter. And, the case would be resolved without the need for a jury trial.

Thoman called Dixie's lawyer later that same week. The prosecutor requested formal confirmation that Dixie accepted the plea by the following Monday. As an added courtesy, Thoman notified Judge Smith of the plea offer.

Oddly, Monday came and went without a returned phone call or any response from Steensland. Tuesday came and went without a phone call or a response from Dixie's lawyer. Thoman wondered what was up.

On Wednesday, he picked up his phone and placed a call to Steensland, Dixie's lead public defender.

"When I asked for the confirmation that Dixie Shanahan would plead guilty to voluntary manslaughter, he simply said that she decided she would not," Thoman said.

Dixie Shanahan listens to advice from her lead public defender, Greg Steensland, at right, during her first-degree murder trial at the Shelby County Courthouse in Harlan, Iowa. Photo courtesy of The Des Moines Register

At the end of the day, Dixie made the decision herself

to reject the prosecutor's plea bargain offer. She was perfectly fine with putting her fate in the hands of the Shelby County jury system. She did not believe that a hometown jury would ever convict her of first-degree murder, let alone voluntary manslaughter, if given that option.

On the contrary, the prosecutor was not offended that Dixie had rejected his plea offer.

"I was actually somewhat relieved, because I felt she had committed murder, or at least I could make a very strong case that she had," Thoman said.

* * *

As the case neared trial, Dixie's plight continued to garner major news media attention throughout the Heartland.

Television crews from Des Moines and Omaha, Nebraska, descended upon Harlan, the Shelby County seat, to cover the courtroom proceedings.

Renowned Nebraska investigative television journalist Joe Jordan was responsible for covering the notorious murder trial for Omaha television station KMTV.

According to Jordan, his crew converged on Defiance, yet astonishingly, it was pretty much impossible to get anybody to go on camera for even a short television interview about the case.

"No one around Defiance wanted to discuss it," said

Jordan, who now serves as managing editor and investigative reporter for NebraskaWatchdog.org, an investigative news website. "That was highly unusual."

On April 21, 2004, Dixie Shanahan's jury trial in the Iowa District Court of Shelby County officially got underway in the Shelby County Courthouse in downtown Harlan.

Charles L. Smith III stayed on as the presiding judge over the historic western Iowa murder case. Unlike neighboring states, such as Illinois and Nebraska, Iowa's courtrooms allowed news media cameras inside their courtrooms. Iowa's friendly open-access policies allowed Court TV to broadcast State v. Dixie Lynn Shanahan into the television sets of its legions of faithful viewers from across the country.

Dixie Shanahan entered the courtroom as a new woman.

In the days leading up to the trial, Dixie and her boyfriend, Jeff Duty, had married. The promise of a new life together relied entirely on the results of the case at hand.

Charles Thoman, the prosecutor, had first crack at presenting his opening statement to the newly seated twelve-member jury.

After he stood, he panned the wooden jury box. He advised the jury that Dixie Lynn Shanahan was on trial for first-degree murder. He read from the formal trial information.

"Dixie Shanahan on or about the month of August 2002, in Shelby County, Iowa, did willfully, deliberately, and with premeditation and malice aforethought kill Scott Shanahan. To this charge, the defendant has entered a plea of not guilty," Thoman told the courtroom.

Thoman maintained eye contact with the jury. He tried his best to connect with all twelve, individually. He appealed to their righteousness, humanity, and sense of decency.

"It's at this point that I have a chance to outline for you and hopefully in plain English what evidence you can expect to hear during the course of this trial that will prove the defendant's guilt of those charges," Thoman told jurors.

"Ladies and gentlemen," Thoman declared, "this is really a case about choices and the choice made by this defendant in this case. At some point in time between August 26, 2002, and most likely September 1 of 2002, this defendant, Dixie L. Shanahan, took a loaded shotgun, approached, and came upon her husband, who was sleeping at the time, opened the shotgun's action to make sure that it was loaded, slammed the bolt home, leveled the gun at the back of his head, and fired a 20-gauge shotgun blast into the back of Scott's head, killing him instantly. I expect you'll find this from the evidence beyond a reasonable doubt."

Clearly, AG Thoman had a difficult job ahead of him. He was working on behalf of the State of Iowa to bring justice to Scott Shanahan. This was the same Scott Shanahan who, when alive, was quite a scoundrel and an ogre around his home. The man mercilessly beat his wife. He lived to terrorize her, day and night.

"Their marriage was a troubled marriage," Thoman conceded. "There is no doubt about it. We've talked about it during the jury selection, both privately and out here in open court, and yes, there were some difficulties."

Trial evidence would demonstrate that Scott Shanahan liked being a loner.

"He did smoke marijuana. There was marijuana found in the house when it was searched," Thoman offered. "He was possessive of his things. Maybe had a short fuse. He was probably a person that most of us would say was hard to like."

At the outset of this highly sensationalized murder trial, the prosecutor slowly and methodically walked the jury through not just one or two, but all three instances when the Shelby County Sheriff's Office was summoned to a contentious domestic violence spat involving Scott Shanahan being the abuser and his wife, Dixie Shanahan, being the victim.

"The sheriff's office takes these kinds of calls seriously, and they have some obligations that they have to fulfill," Thoman explained.

Fortunately, none of the abuse put Dixie's life in danger, jurors learned.

"Don't get me wrong, that does not make what Scott did to this defendant right, but luckily they were not serious injuries. They were not permanent or disfiguring in any way," Thoman stressed.

Thoman foreshadowed for the jury how Dixie Shanahan and her defense team planned to argue that Dixie killed her husband during a courageous and valiant act of self-defense.

He also knew that the defense might cite an abundance of instances when Dixie's husband left her terribly beaten and battered, including several additional incidents that were never, ever, reported by her to law enforcement.

"You'll see what happened when she reported it," the prosecutor advised. "If there were other instances of domestic abuse, you'll have to listen to that testimony. They'll obviously urge that it supports a claim of self-defense. But, I ask you to listen to all of the evidence. Listen to the court's instructions and then at the end of this case, when it's your turn to deliberate and reach a verdict in this case, I'm going to argue that and tell you that she did not act in self-defense. That she is guilty of murder in the first degree, and I'll ask you to return that verdict."

Thoman was finished.

He had painted a dark and disturbing portrait of Dixie Shanahan as being a ruthless, dirty-rotten, premeditated killer. If jurors believed the prosecution's theory and supporting evidence, then Dixie Shanahan was on her way to a one-way ticket to the Iowa penitentiary for the rest of her natural life.

Dixie, though, exhibited the utmost confidence in her two court-appointed public defenders, lead counsel Greg Steensland and co-counsel Charles Fagan. Steensland and Fagan were not rookies. Both men had been involved in numerous other Iowa murder cases and jury trials during their legal careers as state-appointed public defenders.

* * *

The next morning, at 9:05 a.m. Steensland delivered the opening statement on behalf of his client. Jurors listened intently. Everyone in the jury box knew that this murder trial was not a case of who did it. The defense did not dare try to float any crazy or ridiculous theories suggesting that one of Scott's many enemies around Defiance was responsible for his slaying or that perhaps he had died from a suicide.

To a large extent, Steensland began his opening statement by reiterating a key theme noted in the prosecutor's statement.

"Yesterday, you were told that this is a case about choices," Steensland reminded the jury. "And to a certain extent, I would agree. This is a case about choices but it's a case about what happens to those choices."

Steensland continued, delivering a passionate and heartfelt plea. He hoped to sway the hearts and minds of jurors to examine the evidence from his client's vantage point, from all that she had been through in her chaotic, difficult, and often dreadful life.

"It's a case about abuse. It's a case about control. It's a case about justification and how choices in a person's life can be reduced to virtually no choice at all," Steensland declared loudly.

Until now, jurors sat and wondered silently amongst themselves whether or not Dixie Shanahan, herself, would take to the witness stand and testify on her own behalf. Quite often, defense attorneys refuse to put their clients on the stand in a murder trial for good reasons. A very good prosecutor usually rips the defendant apart and leaves them humiliated after pointing out a number of glaring inconsistencies in their statements and actions.

But, this murder trial would not be normal.

Dixie's lawyer promised Shelby County's newly seated panel that Dixie would absolutely testify in her own defense.

"You will be hearing from Dixie Shanahan personally," Steensland alerted the jury. "She will be testifying in this case and tell you what happened, in her life and on that day. So that will not be a mystery to you. You'll hear it straight from her."

Moreover, Dixie would tell the jurors how she grew up in a home that was full of abuse, including sexual abuse perpetuated by her own stepfather, Steensland warned the courtroom.

"Unfortunately, Dixie is going to have to tell you things about her life that she would just as soon nobody ever had to hear about," Steensland explained. "But, in the context of this case, it has to be."

As for the murder victim, Scott Shanahan treated his wife like just one of his many possessions, jurors were told.

"He valued his possessions. And, you'll hear evidence that it was his house, his car, his things. There's never any reference to their home, their things, their family. It's his. That was his mindset. It's his. Very, very possessive, including his wife, Dixie. She was just another possession to him," Steensland declared.

Switching gears, Steensland focused on the guts of the case. He realized the jury had plenty of questions. He knew they would shake their heads and wonder in sheer amazement about how in the world Dixie Shanahan fatally shot her husband and then kept his body stored in their back bedroom for so much time. He assured jurors that Dixie killed her husband because she thought that Scott would kill her otherwise.

"She'd had enough," Steensland insisted. "Then, she closes the door. And, she closes the door as much as a person that's been under that kind of control can in their life. … And, you do odd things. You do things that look completely inappropriate, like leaving a body in a room for over a year."

Dixie was not an attorney. She did not know the legal definition of justification. Rather, she feared that she would go to jail for killing a man, her lawyer argued forcefully.

"If this was a premeditated murder, ladies and gentlemen, would the body stay in a room for a year?" Steensland pondered. "Would you have found a way to dispose of it?"

Based on her turbulent marriage, Dixie was left with only one choice in her life.

"And, that was to kill him," Steensland proclaimed. "The law says that's justified. It's not pretty. It's not nice. It's not what we want, but it's justified. At the end of the case, I'll be asking you to return a verdict of not guilty. Thank you."

As he watched the jury trial unfold from his seat in the cozy courtroom gallery, Joe Jordan, the distinguished Omaha television journalist, was not quite sure what the outcome of Dixie's murder case was going to be.

"It was clearly a fascinating case," Jordan said. "It was certainly a huge case in the Omaha area, and I think the case showed that domestic violence is something that needs to be looked at. And then, there were the bizarre elements and the bizarre nature of the case. It was so unusual to have a body in a house for fourteen months. That was just unbelievable."

Chapter 15 — Dixie on the Stand

The trial of Dixie Shanahan consisted of many of the usual and presumed witnesses. Shelby County Sheriff's officials, Iowa Division of Criminal Investigation officials, the state's chief medical examiner, several of Scott and Dixie Shanahan's neighbors and acquaintances from around the Defiance area.

One of the most unusual witnesses called to testify was Robert McConnell.

He was the man employed by Defiance, Iowa, to read the water meters in town.

Thoman asked him to tell the jury about his observations in the backyard of the Scott and Dixie Shanahan home.

"When you read that water meter during the winter of 2002 and 2003 at the Shanahan residence," the prosecutor asked, "did you ever notice anything out of the ordinary?"

"Yeah," McConnell testified. "That window right above the meter was open. They're awning-type windows, and it was cranked wide open."

As the jurors listened intently, Thoman inquired why the open window at the Shanahan property left such a distinct memory on the town's one and only meter reader.

"Well," McConnell responded, "It's pretty unusual that time to have a window open in the winter like that."

As the jury trial moved along, there was one jailhouse snitch, a woman from Council Bluffs, who was a convicted felon and methamphetamine dealer.

She was a former cellmate of Dixie's at the Shelby County Jail. It seems like you can't have a high-profile murder trial without at least one jailhouse snitch stepping forward to rat out a cellmate to cut a special deal to save their own hide. In this case, the snitch's contribution for the prosecution seemed rather miniscule.

Don't misunderstand, all of the witness testimony put forth by the prosecution and the defense was valuable and insightful for the jury to hear, weigh, and digest in their final analysis.

But at the end of the day, this jury trial really boiled down to the testimony and believability of one star witness, the defendant herself, Dixie Lynn Shanahan, age thirty-six.

If she came off as honest and convincing, the jury would probably find her not guilty of murder. To convict Dixie of murder, Iowa Assistant Attorney General Charles Thoman needed to identify flaws, serious flaws, in Dixie's trial testimony regarding Scott Shanahan's untimely death at age forty within the couple's home.

Clearly, the prosecutor, not the defendant, had the more daunting task. The defendant was presumed to be not guilty, and the prosecution needed to prove she was guilty of murder beyond a reasonable doubt. The bar for the prosecution was, indeed, quite high.

* * *

With Dixie on the witness stand, her friendly and easy-going criminal defense attorney, Greg Steensland, gently guided her along. He handed her the photos of all three of her children. One photo showed her oldest son, Zachary, who was almost eight. Another photo showed her middle child, daughter Ashley, age six. The third photo showed her baby girl, Brittany, who had just turned thirteen months.

Suddenly, Thoman spoke up in the courtroom.

"Your honor, I would object as irrelevant and immaterial to any issue before the court."

Judge Smith disagreed. He allowed the defendant's lawyer to introduce the family photos of Dixie's three young children as evidence exhibits in her murder trial.

"The objection is overruled," Smith told the jurors.

Rather quickly, the trial heated up. Steensland turned his attention to the late summer months of 2002. By that point, Scott's personality had undergone a recent and sudden transformation. When her husband was not home, Dixie poked around the property. She came across a bag of marijuana that her husband had stashed out in his shed. Dixie despised drugs, so she went ahead and flushed the drugs down one of their toilets.

A couple weeks later, Scott and Dixie, along with their young son and daughter, went on a short vacation to Lake Okoboji, which is a popular outdoor swimming and boating recreation area for residents of Iowa and Nebraska during the summer time. At the cabin, Dixie turned on the morning cartoons for her children. This woke Scott up and turned him into a red ball of fire. He pounded Dixie and demanded that she turn off the television, so he could get more restful sleep.

When Scott later discovered that his wife had flushed his marijuana drugs down their toilet, he thumped her even more.

"Towards the end of August, how was your relationship with Scott?" Steensland quizzed his client.

"Very, very rocky," Dixie responded. She endured regular physical beatings, three or four times per week.

"I'd have bruises everywhere."

The jurors listened intently as Steensland floated his client's version of events that led to the deadly shooting.

There was lots of intrigue building in the courtroom.

"In late August," Dixie's public defender asked, "was there a discovery that was made by you?"

"Yes, there was," Dixie confirmed.

"What was that?"

"That I was pregnant again."

"Did you tell Scott?"

"At first, no, but then, yes, ultimately, I did. He went ballistic."

"What did he tell you to do?"

"Have an abortion."

"What did you tell him?"

"No way."

An epic battle ensued.

Most of Dixie and Scott's vicious fights and screaming matches were resolved quickly. But, this fight festered. It lingered for approximately three whole days.

During that period, Scott fumed. Dixie steamed, as well. Emotions were intense. Scott was still refusing to work, let alone even bother go out looking for a job. Dixie did not have a job, either, at the time, since she had her hands full raising their two young kids. And now, the two broke parents, who fought and bickered constantly, were on the verge of having a third child. They had bills to pay. There were groceries to buy. Foremost, they had a monthly mortgage on the property that Scott inherited from his late mother, back in 1994.

And so, the house at 206 Third Avenue had essentially turned into a giant tinder box. The ranch and the personalities inside the home were bound to explode.

* * *

According to Dixie's trial testimony, these are the key events that transpired during the morning of August 30, 2002:

Dixie awoke that morning at 6:30 a.m. Next, she got both her children up. She helped her son, Zachary, get dressed for grade school. Timing was critical because the school bus rolled through the neighborhood at 7:02 a.m. sharp.

"Where was Scott?" Dixie's lawyer asked.

"In bed."

Dixie sent her son into the master bedroom, the room in the far northeast corner of the house. The little boy tried to wake his father before leaving for school.

But, Scott bristled. Scott the sloth just stayed in bed and continued to enjoy his deep sleep. As far as Dixie was concerned, there was no time to dillydally. She put her son on his school bus, and Zachary rode off to school without any acknowledgement from his possessive and volatile, hot-headed father.

Then, all of a sudden, it seemed like a tornado blew through the home on Third Avenue.

“Scott came out of the bedroom and flew into a rage because I didn’t make sure he was awake when Zachary got on the school bus,” Dixie testified.

“What did he do?” her defense lawyer asked.

“Pulled me by the hair and started beating me in the stomach.”

Scott’s screaming grew louder. Dixie ushered their daughter, Ashley, over to a friend’s house about two blocks away.

The domestic violence escalated. Dixie retreated into the garage. She intended to get into their car and scram. But Scott stopped her cold in her tracks.

“He ultimately followed me out and said there was no f’in’ way I was gonna leave and take the car. And he took the keys,” Dixie testified.

Suddenly, the fierce and raving lunatic husband knocked Dixie down against the concrete floor of the garage.

Next, “he drug me by my hair back into the house,”

Dixie testified. "I had chunks of that hair that he had pulled out."

Scott hollered. He punched his wife. His blows struck her stomach.

"I'm gonna kill this baby. You're not having this baby," Dixie recalled him saying.

Dixie fell down again. She cried profusely. A few minutes later, her husband reemerged. He clutched his trusty 16-gauge J.C. Higgins model shotgun.

"He's just shaking and telling me that I'm an S.O.B. I'm a bitch. I'm every name, you name it, I was called it," Dixie testified.

Dixie writhed in pain. She was beaten down and humiliated. Moments later, she watched in horror as her beast of a husband reached into one of the top shelves of their kitchen cupboard.

"He put shells in the gun," she testified. "I only knew that he put two different ones in it."

"How did you know that?" her lawyer wondered.

"Because I seen him do it. He pointed it at me and told me that 'This day is not over yet. I will kill you.'"

She escaped to a living room chair. But, her escape was brief. Scott lunged after her. He resumed giving her another beat down because he felt she was a lousy and worthless wife. He proclaimed that he planned to kill her and the unborn baby, though, apparently, not quite yet.

"This day is not over yet," Scott supposedly warned her again.

From there, Scott retreated into the kitchen. He yanked two of their phone jacks out of the walls. He carried both phones back into the master bedroom. And there Scott stayed in his lair.

At that point, Dixie testified, she made up her mind to alert the authorities. This would have marked her first time of contacting Shelby County law enforcement deputies in close to two full years. Her last contact was in the form of that letter that she had written from Texas. That was the letter she had mailed to the Shelby County Attorney's Office announcing that she was refusing to cooperate in their upcoming felony domestic abuse trial against her husband.

If she had testified, the domestic violence case against Scott would have been a slam dunk. Scott would have gone to prison. Dixie could have moved on with her life.

But, none of that mattered now.

And none of those thoughts raced through Dixie's head during the morning of August 30, 2002. In this instant, she did not dart for the front door to borrow a phone from one of her trusted neighbors. Rather, she leapt from the living room chair and scampered down the hallway. She darted straight toward the very same room where her ferocious husband was lurking.

"I went to the bedroom to get the phone," Dixie

testified.

One of their phones was beside the bed.

Of course, Scott was back in that bedroom, too. He was in quite a fury. When Dixie walked into the master bedroom, it was as if she had startled a giant grizzly bear while it was eating out of a garbage bin. He gazed at her with a look of death.

"He started coming at me," Dixie testified.

Dixie saw Scott's shotgun propped up against the wall. The weapon was within Scott's reach. Now, Dixie had no experience handling guns. Scott's guns were his guns. His weapons intimidated, controlled, and frightened his petrified wife.

In a flash, Dixie put her life on the line. She lunged for Scott's loaded shotgun.

"Did you grab the gun?" her lawyer asked.

"Yes, I did."

"Did you shoot it?"

"Yes."

"At that point in time, Dixie, did you think you had any other way to save yourself and your unborn child?"

"No, I did not."

Bang.

Indeed, Dixie's one-and-only shot struck her target, the man she once loved, the man she had given nineteen years of her life. The same man she had fled from several times, only to be wooed back to Defiance by his charming personality and promises to change his ways, to seek help, to seek counseling, to attend batterer's education classes, to become a faithful and caring husband, among other great things, to keep Dixie by his side.

After the gun smoke had cleared, Dixie sat down and buried her hands in her face. Her mind replayed the episode again and again. The house was eerily silent. No more screams and yells. Finality and reality sank in. She was now a thirty-five-year-old widow, with two young children and a third child due in March. On the bright side, Scott Shanahan was not going to magically jump out of bed and harm Dixie ever again. Her beatings were over. Her husband could no longer torture her, humiliate her, or tie Dixie up in their basement and threaten to leave her there until the end of time.

Dixie was liberated. She was a new woman. And yet, she was afraid, perhaps more afraid than any period in her troubled and tormented life. She agonized about what she had done.

"What was going through your mind?" Steensland wondered.

"That I was gonna go to jail because I had just shot somebody."

Eventually, Dixie went back into the master bedroom

to gather up the telephones. She also retrieved the shotgun. Out of all the locations in her home, Dixie decided that the best place to store the loaded weapon was in one of the closets of her children's bedroom.

* * *

Originally, Dixie testified that her motive for confronting her husband inside their bedroom was to grab one of the phones. That way, Dixie could notify the cops that Scott had beaten her like a rag doll all that morning. But now that she had shot Scott, different thoughts raced through Dixie's head.

"I pretty well sat in the chair the whole day just wondering what I was gonna do," she testified.

Here's what she decided not to do that day: She refused to alert the Shelby County authorities that her husband was dead in their bedroom and that she had just shot him.

Instead, the northeast bedroom became a morbid sanctuary. A not-quite-forty-year-old dead man's corpse was hidden underneath the covers and blankets. Scott was left there to rot and decay, day after day, week after week, month after month, old calendar to new calendar.

"I shut the doors on the bedroom," Dixie testified.

Smartly, Dixie decided to take special precautions to at least mask the smell of Scott's decomposing body. This made some sense, since she was going to continue to share her home with the man she had just shot to death.

She lined the carpet underneath the wooden master bedroom door with a long bath towel. The towel fulfilled its function. It successfully blocked the smell of Scott's decomposing body from seeping underneath the shut door and emitting awful odors throughout the rest of the ranch.

For good measure, Dixie put a couple of air fresheners on the carpet right up against the bedroom door. That door also was locked shut from the inside, and then a clothing hamper was lodged up against the second door, the one between the hallway bathroom and the master bedroom.

Between the locked door, the blocked door, the long, rolled-up bath towel, and the pair of scented air fresheners, Dixie had created a nice fortress to repel any odors of her dead husband's remains. Dixie also kept the bedroom window cranked wide open. That way, the pleasant summer breeze would help circulate air into the northeast corner bedroom — and so would the bone-chilling cold, brisk winter winds that blew through Iowa during the months of November and December, along with January and February of 2003.

"Did you ever do anything about Scott being in that back bedroom?" her lawyer asked.

"No."

"Did you ever tell anybody?"

"No."

In time, plenty of people asked about her husband Scott's whereabouts.

"I told them he went to Atlantic," she testified.

"You lied, didn't you?" her lawyer prodded.

"Yes, I did, because I didn't want to go to jail."

Chapter 16 — Cross-Examination

Assistant Iowa Attorney General Charles Thoman knew that Dixie's plea for sympathy might play well with a hometown jury. After all, very few people around Shelby County were sad to wake up and realize that Scott Shanahan was dead. And yet, Thoman had to dutifully carry out his assignment from the state of Iowa of bringing justice to the homicide victim, Scott Shanahan.

So far, the jury had only heard Dixie Shanahan's teary-eyed and emotional ordeal from her seat in the front of the courtroom. All of those questions were delicately asked by her defense attorney, Greg Steensland. There also was a box of white tissues for Dixie to use to wipe her teary eyes.

Thoman expected the cross-examination would be very difficult for him. He knew that he needed to treat her with fairness on the witness stand, but raise questions about her credibility.

"I will admit that I was surprised by her claim that

Scott Shanahan lunged at her and/or the shotgun, since the photographic evidence, in my mind, clearly showed that he was asleep when she shot him," Thoman recalled. "I felt this ruined her credibility in the jury's eyes."

That day in the Shelby County Courthouse, Thoman turned a masterful and marvelous performance.

Thoman began by asking Dixie about this supposed brutal fight on the morning of August 30, 2002, prior to the deadly shooting.

Dixie insisted that she suffered bruises on her stomach and legs. She had black eyes. A clump of her long dark hair was yanked out while they fought in the garage.

"Both eyes were black?" Thoman followed up.

"Yes."

Furthermore, Scott had beaten her stomach area for at least a couple days prior.

"These were hard blows?" Thoman wondered.

"Yes."

"You're telling this jury they were very extremely forceful blows?"

"Yes."

"And, yet, Brittany was born?"

"Yes, she was."

On the witness stand, Dixie acknowledged that her baby girl was born just fine in March of 2003. The girl had no health problems or complications.

Continuing along that path, Thoman tried to plant the seed in the minds of the fair-minded and impartial jury that Dixie Shanahan, though clearly a longtime domestic-violence victim, was prone to totally making up wild stories to exaggerate her abuse, too.

"You've admitted exaggerating the extent of your injuries in the past, haven't you?" Thoman asked her.

"I have wrote that they were exaggerated, yes."

From there, Thoman had a field day tearing the witness apart regarding her numerous lies about her dead husband's whereabouts. The methodical prosecutor reminded Dixie of her conversation with Shelby County Sheriff's Deputy John Kelly in the driveway of her home, back in late July of 2003.

"You told John Kelly he was in Atlantic," Thoman alerted Dixie.

"In Atlantic, yes, that is where I told everybody he was at."

But back in October of 2002, Dixie told Stephen Johnson a much different story. Johnson was the Council Bluffs man who traveled to Defiance to pay Dixie eight hundred dollars to buy one of Scott's classic cars, plus some of his tools.

"You told Mr. Johnson, remember the car nut from Council Bluffs? You told him that Scott had ran off with a woman?" Thoman reminded Dixie.

"Yes, I did."

Moreover, Dixie also told others in Defiance an even different story.

"And, you told another one of these witnesses that he was living in Atlantic with his drug dealer?"

"Yes."

"That's another lie?"

"Yes."

"So we have lies about where he was at?"

"Yes."

"And, lies about what had happened to him?"

"Yes."

After killing her husband, Dixie had gone ahead and sold off Scott's prized tools. She also sold his classic cars, his old farm tractor, and his snowmobile.

"Netted about ten thousand four hundred dollars out of all that?" Thoman inquired.

"Yes."

Dixie put the proceeds into a money order. She sent it to one of her sisters in Texas.

"Then you didn't have to report it to anybody up here, did you?" Thoman pressed.

"No, I did not."

Soon after, Dixie sought public welfare from the state of Iowa. Her welfare application indicated that Dixie was a single parent and pretty much dirt poor.

And then, there was that fateful day when Iowa authorities finally searched the Shanahan property.

Back on October 20, 2003, Sheriff Gene Cavenaugh and Iowa DCI Special Agent David Jobes gave Dixie one final opportunity to come clean and level with them about her missing husband before they invaded her home and executed a search warrant.

On that occasion, she told the two investigators that her husband had run off with a forty-year-old, heavy-set blonde woman.

"And this is after Scott is dead and lying in that northeast bedroom at the time, right?" Thoman inquired.

"Yes."

"Well, you didn't tell the sheriff that you shot him, did you?"

"No, I never told him, no."

Instead, Dixie told the sheriff and special agent that Scott had dropped by the home on three different occasions with the heavy-set blonde to retrieve some clothes and fetch some of his favorite musical CDs.

"All false?" Thoman asked.

"Yes."

* * *

Regarding the purported events of August, 30, 2002, the astute, experienced prosecutor decided to pull out an obscure, yet noteworthy, clue to significantly undermine Dixie's earlier testimony.

He remembered how Dixie testified that she basically buried her hands in her head and sat in the living chair of her home, all day long, contemplating what she had done.

"You shot and killed Scott Shanahan about what time of the day on August 30?" Thoman inquired.

Surely before noon, Dixie contended.

"So after you shot and killed Scott Shanahan and were so upset, you got in the car and drove up to the No-Frills store?" Thoman wondered.

There was a break in the cross-examination as Thoman presented the courtroom with a check that Dixie had written on August 30, 2002. The check was made out to the No-Frills grocery store about thirteen miles up the road from Defiance, on the north edge of Denison.

"Yes, I did," she conceded.

"Wrote a check?"

"Yes."

The discovery that Dixie forged a check on an August 30, 2002, grocery store excursion up the road in Denison served an important purpose for the prosecutor. First of all, Thoman had not been convinced that Dixie had actually killed her husband that particular day. Thoman figured the killing may have happened anytime between August 26 and September 1. On the other hand, if Scott was killed on August 30, 2002, Dixie's decision to go on a shopping spree played exactly into the prosecution's deck of cards.

"I had in my files all of the forged checks that defendant Dixie Shanahan had written after Scott's murder," Thoman said in an interview. "I knew that the first one was written on the date that she was claiming she killed Scott. I thought this tied in perfectly with my economic theory — that she did not kill him in some kind of battered woman/self-defense scenario, but she killed him because his money had run out and she had no more use for him.

"Her acts in killing Scott in the morning, driving up to Denison a couple hours later, going on a shopping spree at the store in Denison and forging Scott's signature to a check to pay for the goods — while Scott's dead body was lying at home in bed — were not the actions of a battered woman forced to commit homicide. Rather, they were the actions of a cold and calculating person."

During Dixie's trial, Thoman advised the jurors that back on October 16, 2002 — more than five full weeks after Scott was slain — Dixie went ahead and penned a letter to the bank handling the mortgage on the Third Avenue house.

Thoman made her read the letter out loud in the courtroom.

"Scott Shanahan sent that letter?" Thoman asked.

"No."

"You did?"

"Yes, I did. October the 16th."

"Another instance in which you seem to be in control of things, is that right?"

This time, Dixie grew perturbed with the prosecutor's assertion.

"The reason this letter was wrote was because we was four months behind and there was a foreclosure. It wasn't to have my name put on this account. It was just so that I could talk to the people concerning the account."

Slowly, Thoman turned his attention to the body in the bedroom. He asked how often Dixie changed out the candles to mask the odor of her decaying husband on the other side of the shut door.

"Probably three times in a year."

“How often did you change the towel?”

“I didn’t.”

She also admitted that she put the large piece of cardboard up against the bedroom door.

“It was a TV box. My kids had got a TV for Christmas, and the box was there because they played with it and they would take it from that spot right there to play rodeo with.”

The prosecutor tried pressing Dixie to admit that she surely had gone into the bedroom on many occasions, but Dixie adamantly maintained that she had not set foot in the back bedroom. Quite frankly, she was probably telling the truth.

Showing that Dixie had lied about Scott’s disappearance and the overdrawn bank account was meaningful, but the clock was ticking on Thoman to deliver a couple of serious technical knockout blows to convince the jury that Dixie had committed murder.

For the prosecutor, it defied logic for Dixie to enter the bedroom of her evil and vicious husband just moments after Scott had finished thumping her mercilessly that very same morning.

“What else am I supposed to do?” she whimpered.

“How about standing up, walking out of the house, and calling the sheriff and getting some help?” Thoman offered. “I just don’t understand why you would go in the bedroom to get the phone when you knew he was in there if he presented that great of danger? Or was he lying in bed? He was, right?"

"Yes, he was."

Suddenly, Thoman remembered that the grisly crime scene photos showed Scott had a pillow between his legs.

"Liked to hug a pillow," Thoman addressed the courtroom, "and a lot of people sleep that way, ma'am. You know, they have an arm around a pillow. They have a pillow between their legs, lying on their side. Scott would sleep that way, wouldn't he?"

"Sometimes, I suppose. Yes."

In addition, her husband often slept wearing his underpants.

"And yet, you're saying you could walk in that bedroom, go over to the phone, take that gun, and shoot him, all while he's awake?" Thoman asked.

"Yes."

Thoman displayed one of the more striking crime-scene photos showing Scott's dead body in the bedroom.

"You've seen this picture, ma'am," Thoman spoke up. "I'm not trying to stun you or anything, but you've seen it, right?"

"Yes, I have."

"You know where the shot struck him, right?"

"In the back of the head, I guess, yes."

Astonishingly, Dixie testified that she never even tried to move the body after the shooting.

"All you did was pull up the sheets?" Thoman inquired.

"Yes."

"Pull up the sheets to cover the body?"

"Yes, I did."

The disturbing and ghastly crime scene photos were taken fourteen months after the actual homicide. These exhibits were the prosecutor's best arsenal of evidence.

"Look at that exhibit, ma'am," Thoman handed Dixie the photos. "That's Exhibit Thirty-three."

Dixie glanced at the photo.

"That's somebody who's asleep," Thoman declared.

The prosecutor's assertion unnerved her.

"No, he was not asleep!" Dixie fired back.

That afternoon in the Shelby County courtroom, Thoman worked like a hammer pounding a steel nail into a wooden board. Like a good carpenter, Thoman wasn't going to finish until he was completely done with the job. After all, the twelve jurors sitting just a few feet away would determine once and for all whether the shooting death of Scott Shanahan was a courageous act of self-defense or a cowardly act of intentional murder.

The prosecutor knew this was murder. The evidence was black and white. There was nothing gray about this crime.

"That's not someone who's reaching for a gun, ma'am," Thoman emphasized in a polite, but firm tone.

"He made a movement. I thought he was coming after me."

"What movement did he make?"

"It was like he was coming, rolling over on the bed."

"Well, when he made a movement for the gun, if you're telling us the truth, he was facing you, not with his back to you."

"I thought he was coming for the gun. I'm not saying where he was at or whatever. I thought he made a movement for the gun, and I wasn't gonna let him do it."

Chapter 17 — The Shotgun

Many defense attorneys are portrayed in the movies and on television dramas as being unscrupulous, lacking ethics or morals, and being willing to do just about anything to get their clients off.

But, Dixie Shanahan's public defender was not a shameless lawyer. Rather, Greg Steensland was one of the most ethical and classy lawyers around in southwestern Iowa. Prior to the trial, Steensland steered the authorities to the elusive shotgun used to kill Scott Shanahan. After consulting with the client, Dixie's defense team revealed to the prosecution where the weapon was located within her home. The shotgun, a 16-gauge J.C. Higgins bolt-action weapon, was then recovered by the Iowa investigators.

The location where Dixie had hidden the weapon, along with the shotgun itself, were key points of contention revealed by the prosecutor during the murder trial.

* * *

At least Dixie had enough smarts to forbid her small children from going inside the northeast bedroom where their father's body continued to rot under the blankets and bed sheets day after day. On the other hand, she decided to hide the loaded shotgun used to kill him inside the children's bedroom closet.

"Why?" Thoman asked.

"Because that's where I put it when I brought it out of there, and the kids slept with me anyhow."

"You didn't think that was a dangerous thing?"

"No, I didn't. Because they never bothered nothing."

Besides, her kids never played in their closet, she testified.

"You weren't worried about the fact that that gun was sitting in that closet?"

"No I was not."

"And, that your children had access to that room?"

"I was not worried about it, no."

Thoman knew that the circumstances of the weapon were paramount to proving his case. When the weapon was finally taken apart by the ballistics experts at the Iowa DCI crime lab, the 16-gauge shotgun bore two completely different caliber shotgun shells. A 20-gauge shotgun shell had been fired successfully, and that was the shell that ended up inside the back of the skull of Scott Shanahan to cause his instantaneous death. Another shell, a 12-gauge shell, was still live and had never been fired. But, that round was jammed and only by taking the shotgun apart could the ballistics expert at the DCI remove that shell from the gun, according to the earlier trial testimony.

"I bet you know why you weren't concerned about that, because you knew it wouldn't fire anymore," Thoman observed.

"No, I did not."

Thoman looked to score more points with the jury.

"You knew that there was a 12-gauge round jammed in the magazine, didn't you?" he asked.

"I knew there were two different bullets in there. Two different colors. But otherwise, no, I did not know that they was in there. I have no clue about a gun. I never fired a shotgun in my life."

Unknowingly, Dixie had walked right into the prosecutor's bear trap.

"That's exactly my point, ma'am," Thoman agreed. "You didn't know how shotguns worked, did you?"

"No, I didn't."

"You didn't know the difference between a 12-gauge shell or a 20-gauge shell or a 16-gauge gun?"

"No, I did not."

"You wouldn't know that that's a problem to try to put 20-gauge ammunition or 12-gauge shells into a 16-gauge gun? You would not know that, would you?"

"No, I would not."

In an act of desperation, Dixie backpedaled. She interjected how she had watched her husband load his shotgun with the two different caliber shotgun rounds and that both were different colors.

Naturally, Thoman didn't believe her story. For all of Scott Shanahan's lousy characteristics, the shooting victim knew a lot about restoring autos, and he also knew a lot about handling firearms. Clearly, Scott knew not to ever load one of his 20-gauge shells and one of his 12-gauge shells into his 16-gauge shotgun.

"Somebody that knows guns would know right away that's something you don't do," Thoman stressed.

* * *

As if Dixie's time on the witness stand wasn't contentious enough, Thoman made it a point to remind Dixie of the many squandered opportunities that she had been afforded to escape the violence and the abuse.

Bottom line, she didn't have to take matters into her own hands and kill her husband in a cruel, cold-blooded fashion.

On three separate occasions, the Shelby County

Sheriff's Office and the county attorney's office had indeed stepped up to the plate on her behalf when Dixie had contacted them. The local prosecutors and sheriff's deputies had been diligent and conscientious, yet she refused to testify against her lousy, good-for-nothing spouse, even though her testimony would have been pivotal to sending him to prison, perhaps for a long time.

Thoman told the jury that by 2002, money problems between Scott and Dixie had pushed Dixie over the edge, and that was what led to her breaking point.

"And then you started thinking by that time that you really did resent Scott. You'd had it, right?"

"I had had it with his beating, yes."

"Especially, when there is no money, nothing to help support you?"

Dixie scoffed at the prosecutor's inference that she killed her husband over money squabbles.

"I was with him thirteen years before he ever had a dime," Dixie snapped. "So that has no bearing on his money."

When Dixie pointed that shotgun at her husband and let go of the trigger, she closed her eyes and shot, she testified under cross-examination.

Thoman was aghast. He hadn't heard that story out of Dixie's mouth before.

"You closed your eyes and shot?" he asked.

"Yes. I'm telling you the truth. I have no reason to sit up here and lie?"

"You don't? You told your lawyer all morning long about how you were worried about going to jail."

"That is true. That is true. I was worried for my kids and myself. I didn't want to have a baby in jail."

At that moment, Thoman didn't have to try too hard to get Dixie to admit that she hoped the blast of the shotgun struck and killed her target.

"Yes, I guess you could say that," Dixie admitted.

Before Thoman wrapped up his relentless grilling of the defendant, he showed Dixie that photograph of her dead husband, in the covers of their bed.

Dixie conceded that she probably shot Scott from a distance of eighteen inches or less. Initially, she claimed she shot him from at least three to four feet away.

"Asleep in bed?" Thoman inquired.

Thoman's question was more of a bold proclamation for the rest of the courtroom rather than a direct yes or no question for Dixie. By now, the facts of the case were becoming clearer to everyone who was paying attention to all of the riveting trial testimony.

"No, not asleep in bed!" Dixie retorted.

* * *

Dixie's public defender, Greg Steensland, had one last time to salvage his client's testimony. The premise of the entire murder trial rested on Dixie's argument that she was within her legal right to shoot and kill her husband.

"Dixie, after Scott was shot, what was it you were trying to accomplish with your life?" her lawyer asked.

"To make my life normal."

The focus turned back to the fateful events of August 30, 2002.

"Tell the jury, again, what happened and what was going through your mind?"

"I just wanted my life to be normal."

In her mind, Dixie had no other alternative than to fire the fatal shotgun blast into the back of her husband's skull and be done with Scott Shanahan.

"Is it what you wanted to do?" her lawyer asked.

"No, it's not."

"Is it what you felt you had to do?"

"Yes, it is."

* * *

Dixie's arch agitator, prosecutor Charles Thoman, still had one more final crack at the defendant. She agreed that her husband was laying in the bed at the time she darted into the bedroom.

“And if he had fallen asleep,” Thoman began, “he wouldn’t have heard you leave, would he?”

“No, he would not have.”

Thoman asked if Scott was facing the gun.

“No, I don’t say facing the gun,” Dixie backpedaled. “He was moving and I felt at that point in time that if I didn’t get to that gun, he would have.”

But, the crime scene and autopsy photos made it clear as day that Dixie fatally shot her husband in the bed from behind.

“He was not facing you when you shot,” Thoman declared.

“No, but he did move, and I did feel that my life was in danger. The man had already pointed a gun at me twice that day. I had no reason, in my mind, to not believe that he would hurt me at that point.”

And with that, Thoman finished up his punishing examination of the defendant.

He made one brief but lasting declaration. It was a statement the Iowa assistant attorney general hoped would resonate and stick with the minds of all twelve of the jurors.

“He was sleeping ma’am.”

"No, he was not," Dixie fired back.

Thoman was done.

"No further questions, your honor."

* * *

It was hard to know what was going through the heads of the twelve western Iowa jurors. They had just absorbed all of the emotional and grilling testimony from murder defendant Dixie Shanahan. Duty requires jurors to basically sit stone-faced and absorb all of the trial evidence like a sponge. They are discouraged from giving visible reaction to the lawyers' actions and the witnesses' remarks. Once the trial has concluded, then the jurors can hash out their reactions behind closed doors and argue and bicker amongst one another.

Dixie's lawyers wanted the jurors to be moved by Dixie's stomach-turning testimony about her troubled youth, her troubled marriage, and her fear of sharing the same home with her wicked abuser, Scott Shanahan. Their narrative for the jury was that Dixie shot and killed her husband to protect her life and that of her unborn child, Brittany.

When the trial was done, if it was a close call, the defense figured the jury would surely give Dixie the benefit of the doubt.

To bolster the defense and sympathy for Dixie, Laurie Schipper, executive director of the Iowa Coalition Against Domestic Violence in Des Moines, was summoned to the witness stand. The graduate of Iowa State University with a bachelor's in social work had already served as an expert witness in approximately one hundred fifteen different court cases.

When it came to the trial of State v. Dixie Shanahan, Public Defender Steensland hoped that Schipper would eloquently articulate the defense's overarching theme: Dixie's cycle of violence, sadly, was not unique.

Dixie was trapped and had no other viable alternatives to get out of her abusive home life.

The fact that Dixie had left Scott several times during their rocky marriage, only to return to Defiance and reconcile, was not unusual, either.

On average, most women who were caught up in a similar cycle of domestic abuse left and later returned to their spouse between five to seven times, Schipper told the jury.

Eventually, Schipper captured the jury's attention by discussing Stockholm syndrome and how it came to be named after a number of bank robbery hostages in Stockholm, Sweden, who ultimately sympathized and made excuses for their captors.

"They bonded with them, and in fact, two of them went on to become engaged to their captors," Schipper testified.

So how did Stockholm syndrome relate to the trial and plight of Dixie Shanahan?

Schipper had plenty of answers to share with the courtroom.

Many of these brain-washing techniques have been highlighted by the Amnesty International organization, Schipper told the jurors.

"There's this bonding happening, there is certain things that take place, induced exhaustion. So she's either not allowed to sleep, or the beatings create this physical exhaustion. They believe that their survival depends on his survival. Stockholm syndrome is very important in helping us understand battered women's behavior, and it's such a strong dynamic that even after the perpetrator is dead or incarcerated, the battered woman still has a very difficult time talking about the violence, talking bad about him. She still believes he has this sort of omnipotence, that he can hear her. There will still be consequences for disclosing."

When prosecutor Thoman had his chance to cross-examine the defense's domestic violence expert, he did so rather eloquently and with tact.

Schipper conceded that she was first contacted about serving as a defense expert witness about a month before the trial.

"You haven't interviewed the defendant in this case?" Thoman inquired.

"That's correct. I have not."

"Haven't met her?"

"No. Not to my knowledge."

"And if I'm right, you've been discussing battered women and domestic violence in terms of generalities?"

"That's correct."

And with that, Thoman rested.

"Nothing further, your honor."

* * *

Dixie's two lawyers, Steensland and Charles Fagan, lined up nearly twenty different defense witnesses to parade into the courtroom. One by one, they all took the stand in the hopes of convincing jurors that Dixie acted in self-defense.

Here are just a few examples of their remarks about Dixie's dead husband, Scott Shanahan:

"He was evil. He wouldn't keep a job," testified Marc Carl, one of Dixie's neighbors.

"He was violent towards the children. The children were scared to death of him. They started acting up. All he had to do was look at them, and they would go running to Dixie," testified Teresa Merritt, one of Dixie's friends who lived in Omaha.

One of Dixie's former co-workers, Janet Ladehoff of Irwin, Iowa, testified about a conversation she had several years back when Dixie was about eight months pregnant with her second child.

"She had showed me her stomach," Ladehoff testified. "There was some bruising and red marks on her stomach at the time. She had told me that Scott had beat on her stomach. He didn't want the baby, and so he had beat on her."

During the direct examination, Dixie's lawyers asked one of her former co-workers, Cynthia Carpenter, to describe some of the injuries that Dixie suffered.

"Well, besides some of the bruising, the one that stood out the most was when her jaw was broken," Carpenter testified.

Eventually, the witness grew hostile toward the prosecutor when Thoman had his opportunity to cross-examine her.

Thoman vividly remembers the cross-examination. It seemed to be another turning point in the trial.

"She claimed that Scott had broken Dixie's jaw in one incident of domestic violence," Thoman recalled. "As with Dixie, I tried to be very respectful of the witnesses and fair with my cross-examination. With some prodding, she admitted, very reluctantly, that she was wrong when she testified earlier that Scott had broken Dixie's jaw."

In retrospect, Thoman felt that his cross-examination of the witness helped the jurors avoid emotion and sympathy toward the defendant as they carefully weighed all the evidence.

"This gave me the opportunity to follow up by telling

the witness in effect: 'We know Dixie is your friend, we know you never liked Scott, but this is a trial and we only want the truth, the jury only wants the truth, nothing more or less,'" Thoman pointed out.

Chapter 18 — Missed Opportunity

Susan Christensen was called to testify as one of Thoman's rebuttal witnesses, and her testimony played a huge factor in the outcome of the jury trial.

Back on November 19, 1996, when Dixie Shanahan first sought outside legal help to deal with signs of her struggling and failing marriage of less than two years, she went and met with Susan Christensen.

That day, Christensen closed the office and sat down for a one-on-one consultation with Dixie. She told Dixie what her options were. As an assistant Shelby County attorney, Christensen often handled the vast majority of criminal prosecutions in cases involving domestic abuse. She had met with plenty of women in the same boat as Dixie Shanahan during her career.

That fateful day back in 1996, Christensen explained to Dixie that there were plenty of places to turn and get help through the Shelby County justice system. One of those tools was a protection order.

After the meeting ended, Christensen took the initiative to make the Shelby County Sheriff's Office aware of her encounter with Dixie. She was genuinely concerned about Dixie. Christensen had her doubts on whether Dixie would actually follow through and obtain a protection order against her unloving and harmful husband, Scott.

"I wanted our law enforcement to know if they got a call from out there, they should take it very seriously," Christensen testified. "I believed that she was scared and that I was requesting them, because it's a distance away, to be prepared for a call out there."

As time went on, Dixie did not take the initiative to obtain a protection order against Scott.

Christensen went on to share with the jury about the three incidents over the years where Scott was arrested for domestic violence, but each time Dixie backed out on aiding the prosecution.

He basically went unpunished for his awful misdeeds. Talk about getting a lucky break.

From that point forward, Dixie never informed anyone in Shelby County who was empowered to do something on her behalf of any further abuse involving Scott Shanahan.

"Did she ever have any further contact with your office?" Thoman asked Christensen.

"No."

He asked if Dixie ever sought a protection order against Scott.

"No."

He asked if Dixie ever sought criminal charges against Scott.

"No."

He asked if Dixie ever contacted the Shelby County Sheriff's Office for any kind of help.

"No. And I believe they would have contacted me. That's our normal routine."

Thoman utilized Christensen's testimony to not only refute the defense expert witness, Laurie Schipper, but to smash her testimony into a thousand pieces.

"She spoke to us in terms of some generalities," Thoman noted, "and it was at least my impression in listening to her testimony that it was as if there was never any way out of this domestic abuse problem for the woman.

"Has that been your experience as a person who prosecutes domestic abuse and represents women in domestic abuse cases?"

"Absolutely not," the Shelby County assistant prosecutor answered. "I think that is the perception by victims, but it's not reality."

Christensen's answer was not one that the defense was overjoyed in hearing. Her words helped destroy the defendant's courtroom narrative about the troubled and tormented life of Dixie Shanahan. Those facts may have rung true, but Dixie's decision to be helpless rested on her shoulders.

In preparation for the trial, Christensen dug through her prosecutor records to track down her statistics on domestic-abuse cases. From 1998 through April 2004, the Shelby County Attorney's Office had prosecuted about two hundred and thirty five separate domestic violence cases, roughly one case every nine or ten days in Shelby County, she informed the courtroom.

Christensen recited first-hand stories of a few of the many examples of women who also endured loveless marriages fraught with domestic abuse. These women took advantage of Shelby County's elaborate network of resources to help them turn their lives around and end their desperate and scary cycle of violence.

These women did not have to continue to live in fear.

Christensen's message for the jury — and for Dixie — was clear. These women chose a different path, and they wound up with a different outcome, something that Dixie Shanahan could easily have done, as well.

Christensen told the jury about a woman who had been married more than thirty years to a man who beat her quite severely on a regular basis. That man would also burn things that were important to his wife.

"There were scars on her body that I could see when

she came to see me, and she showed me others that would not be visible without her removing some clothing," Christensen recounted.

In that case, the Shelby County Attorney's Office helped the woman obtain a protective order against her abusive husband. Still, the husband violated the protective order a few times. He sent his wife handwritten notes, and put his letters into her mailbox. The woman was persistent in notifying law enforcement of any and all matters of when the protection order was being violated.

In time, the couple divorced.

"And to my knowledge, there have been no further problems in that situation," Christensen told the court.

Another woman was in a situation much like Dixie's. That woman also had three small children at her home. In one classic example of domestic abuse, the abusive husband yanked all of the phones out of the walls on a Halloween night some years ago, and then he pushed his wife out of their house in her pajamas.

"And, when she got in the car to go drive somewhere in the country, he came out and ripped the keys out so she couldn't drive," Christensen recalled.

When Christensen became aware of the woman's dilemma, she knew her role as a prosecutor was to help the woman escape the situation. And, she did just that.

But, that woman's ordeal turned out far less lethal than Dixie's. That woman took advantage of the protection order system over the following year.

"It got hairy many times," Christensen recalled. "In one particular case, her husband faxed a copy of a tombstone with her name on it."

Actually, the picture of the woman's name on the tombstone was great evidence for the prosecutor's office to prove the protective order was violated.

Ultimately, the couple divorced, and the protective order stayed in effect for at least a couple of years.

"And now, that's been dismissed and they live in the same county, they both have remarried other people, and I think are doing well," Christensen testified.

The children also have visitation rights with their dad.

"It's an example where she can be protected and the violence can stop," Christensen testified.

On the contrary, Dixie's case of domestic abuse ended with the murder of her abuser, the jury was reminded.

"I don't believe this case had to end this way," Christensen testified. "I think there were choices that we gave Dixie, in particular, that she chose not to take, and those choices have been proven over and over to be effective if allowed to take their course."

Chapter 19 — Judgment Day

When the trial was over, fair-minded Judge Charles Smith III gave the jurors the rather mundane and tedious instructions. The jury also had the opportunity to consider a number of additional lesser offenses if jurors agreed that Dixie's actions warranted a conviction, but they could not all agree on first-degree murder as the most appropriate charge.

The burden was properly placed upon the State of Iowa and prosecutor Chuck Thoman to prove Dixie's guilt through the evidence beyond a reasonable doubt.

Otherwise, Dixie was presumed to be not guilty of the charges.

"You must determine the defendant's guilt or innocence from the evidence and the law in these instructions," Judge Smith advised the jury.

Joe Jordan, the Omaha television journalist who covered the trial, did not know whether the jury would find her guilty of murder or vote for an acquittal.

"The times you think it can be a slam dunk are the times you sit back after the jury comes back and you go 'Wow! Really?'" Jordan remarked. "You never know what a jury is going to do."

Rightfully so, the jurors followed their judge's words of wisdom and did exactly as they were supposed to do. They were not in total unanimous agreement on the first-degree murder charge. They considered second-degree murder and another much lesser-included felony crime.

Unknown to the jury, the plea bargain had remained on the table for Dixie even during the duration of her jury trial, Judge Smith, now retired, shared in a 2014 interview.

In a best-case scenario, Dixie stood a chance of being released from prison after serving as little as two-and-a-half years of imprisonment on the voluntary manslaughter count.

"Everybody did everything they could in encouraging Dixie to plead guilty to voluntary manslaughter," the judge said. "We twice brought her back into my judge's chambers. She didn't listen. It's my speculation that she was listening to other people, other than (her attorney) Greg Steensland. Greg did a great job, an excellent job, but she just did not want to take the plea."

In the end, Dixie's decision to reject the plea bargain would go down as yet another of her disastrous stumbles and ill-fated decisions in life, right up there with her decision to kill her sleeping husband and hide his body in her bedroom and not tell anyone about it.

In its final analysis, the righteous and fair-minded citizens of Shelby County who comprised the Dixie Shanahan jury brushed aside the hometown sympathy that had swelled up around Iowa due to the intense and high-profile nature of her murder case. Instead, the jury determined that Dixie Lynn Shanahan did not act in self-defense.

She was guilty of second-degree murder.

In retrospect, the jury's decision to convict Dixie of second-degree murder was not an incredible surprise, reflected Jordan.

"Given the way the trial went down, it looked more calculated than a reaction to an incident," he said.

News of Dixie Shanahan's sensational murder conviction even made a blurb in The New York Times on May 1, 2004:

"A woman who fatally shot her husband in August 2002 after what she said was years of abuse was found guilty of second-degree murder. The woman, Dixie Shanahan, a mother of three who left the body of her husband, Scott, in a room of their home in Defiance for more than a year, will be sentenced on May 10. Ms. Shanahan, 36, said she shot her husband as he lunged toward her, but prosecutors say Mr. Shanahan was asleep when he was shot."

In retrospect, Judge Smith noted that he had the authority and power to overturn the jury's verdict or reduce the second-degree murder conviction if the jury had overstepped its bounds during the trial of Dixie Shanahan. But, Judge Smith did not believe the jury was wrong in its determination that Dixie had committed second-degree murder, so he let the conviction stand.

More than ten years later, Smith said he still believes that the jury made the proper verdict.

"She raised self-defense as the defense, but it did not look much like an act of self-defense. The evidence was way to the contrary," Judge Smith said. "The evidence against her was quite strong. It was a second-degree murder."

Of particular note, the witness stand testimony from then-Assistant Shelby County Attorney Susan Christensen, sister of former Shelby County Attorney Jeff Larson, was crucial to the prosecution's case, the judge pointed out.

"Susie's testimony was quite compelling," the retired judge explained. "Jeff Larson and Susie Christensen, they did everything they could for Dixie, but they can't put her in jail to protect her," Smith said, referring to those ill-fated previous instances of when Dixie Shanahan had reported being a victim of abuse at the hands of her husband.

* * *

Dixie wore a pink dress and buttoned-down white

sweater as the handcuffs were tightened around her wrists. Shelby County Sheriff Gene Cavenaugh slowly marched Dixie out of the courthouse and returned her back to the Shelby County Jail. She remained in the jail until the pronouncement of her sentencing about ten days later.

Cavenaugh did not disagree with the jury's verdict. There was no way that the shooting was done in self-defense.

"It was a sad case and sad for the kids in the house. Dixie, no doubt, had been an abused woman and we had gotten her out of the house a number of times. But there is a penalty for killing a person. If you do something like this is, there is a price," Cavenaugh said during a 2014 interview.

Looking back, Dixie Shanahan's murder case was probably the biggest case Cavenaugh handled during his successful Shelby County law enforcement career that spanned thirty-seven years. Because the county was so small, practically everyone was captivated by the Dixie Shanahan murder trial and the fallout of the case.

"Everybody in Defiance and at the Shelby County Sheriff's Office knew that she had been a previous victim of domestic abuse. That was never any question," Cavenaugh said.

"Her first mistake against her was shooting and killing her husband as he slept. Her second mistake was not calling us on the second day. Her third mistake against her was hiding the body and not being truthful. Her fourth mistake was lying to us and the investigators all along during the investigation. She had a lot of strikes already against her."

Dixie's many mistakes in life had compounded like a giant rolling snowball that was cascading down the mountain, until it finally crashed. In the eyes of the criminal justice system, Dixie Shanahan was a notorious convicted murderer.

It was quite clear from the trial testimony that Dixie had plenty of options that she either refused or simply chose to ignore. Plenty of people were in her corner, available to help her, including her siblings in Texas, the Shelby County Sheriff's Office, the Shelby County Attorney's Office, other friends, and conscientious neighbors within the town of Defiance. But, Dixie decided in her own mind to ignore the forces of good that were ready to step in and help her.

Instead, she chose to commit a calculated and cold-blooded killing. In the process, Scott Shanahan died a most peaceful death. He was resting, quite relaxed and comfortable, when Dixie pulled the trigger of Scott's own shotgun. This was one of those shotguns that he just had to keep around his house to serve as a cruel and wicked intimidation force. He took lots of pleasure in scaring and terrifying his wife, Dixie.

But, by the time that law enforcement finally realized what had happened, Scott Shanahan was nothing more than a forty-one-pound body bag of bones, rotting flesh, and biological fluids. His corpse had solidified into a mummified state. Most of his body had been eaten and devoured by thousands of pesky and irritating little blowflies, insects, and maggots.

In the eyes of the law, the eyes of the jury, and the eyes of Iowa's sentencing laws, Dixie needed to be punished for all that she had done. She had given her husband eternal rest. She took away the one and only thing that Scott had — his life. By killing Scott in premeditated fashion, hiding his corpse, and lying to everyone about the crime, Dixie Shanahan had to be punished for her crimes.

* * *

On May 10, 2004, jailers and courthouse security walked Dixie Shanahan back into the Shelby County Courthouse. A sullen Dixie Shanahan sat at the defense table with her lawyer, Greg Steensland. At the opposite table sat Charles Thoman, the assistant Iowa attorney general.

Longtime southwestern Iowa judge Charles Smith III had the formality of sentencing Dixie to prison.

On this morning, there was no point in fiery, passionate oratory remarks or well-thought out eloquent arguments in favor of leniency or mercy by the lawyers or even by Dixie herself. In fact, the sentencing hearing was a bit of a sham.

When Judge Smith asked Dixie if she wanted to address the court before her sentencing, she declined. Following up, the judge asked her attorney, Greg Steensland, the same question.

"It seems like a waste of time the way the law is written," Steensland declared.

Thoman also indicated that he had no additional remarks to make prior to the sentencing.

Judge Smith went ahead and informed Dixie that he had rejected her request to overturn the jury's verdict.

"This isn't to say that the jury or this court isn't sympathetic to the years of abuse you were subjected to, because no human should have to put up with that," Smith told Dixie. "However, the jury decided that the action you took back in 2002, in killing another human being, was not justified, and I cannot and will not disagree."

But, what Smith had to say next were the most lasting and memorable comments of the case. Judge Smith lashed out against the state of Iowa's criminal sentencing guidelines in the hopes of fostering change through the Iowa state legislature.

Fourth District Judge Charles Smith III presided over the jury trial of Dixie Shanahan and was responsible for carrying out her mandatory prison term of fifty years.

"It needs to be said that the mandatory minimum sentencing structure that has been imposed on this court throughout the state of Iowa for this type of offense is, in my opinion, wrong. It may be legal, but it is wrong. The legislature decided some twelve or thirteen years ago that this type of sentence fits all occasions of this offense."

From there, Judge Smith reflected back on his days when he had been a former county prosecutor. Back in the 1970s, the prosecutors and the judges had wide latitude to come up with an appropriate sentence based on other extenuating factors. After all, each murder case is unique.

"By imposing mandatory minimums as severe as this one in this case, a legislature from fifteen years ago is, in effect, sentencing you, without knowing nothing about this case, without trusting the good judgment of the judge in the case, and without trusting the good judgment of the Board of Parole that might consider your case sooner than they will," Smith lamented.

Smith later said in a 2014 interview that he understands why the Iowa legislature enacted certain mandatory prison terms to avoid the possibility of wide sentencing disparities in certain crimes. He wholeheartedly supports the use of a mandatory life prison term for someone convicted of first-degree murder. However, in crimes such as second-degree murder, it seems most appropriate to have a range between twenty to fifty years, for example.

But those days were long gone by the time that a jury of

twelve found Dixie guilty of second-degree murder. In her case, Dixie would receive a flat fifty-year sentence, no matter what the judge thought.

Meanwhile, just west of Iowa, across the Missouri River, judges in Nebraska can have much more latitude in violent-crime sentencing. Someone convicted of second-degree murder in Nebraska can receive a prison sentence ranging anywhere from twenty years to life imprisonment.

"The judge is the one who knows more than anyone else about the case, and yet the legislature is the one that is dictating what the sentence is going to be," Smith said. "I was obviously frustrated. Dixie, obviously, was a battered woman. … I can say that I would have liked to have given her a much lesser sentence. But, my hands were tied."

As Judge Smith correctly pointed out in the courtroom during Dixie's sentencing, her particular case was a tragedy in so many ways. After all, Dixie not only was heading to prison for a very long time, she had also lost the opportunity to raise her three young children. Her kids would be sent away to Texas to live with relatives. Dixie would be stripped of the opportunity to nurture her children and watch them grow up. She would not have the chance to be there to blow out the candles on their birthday cakes or watch them wide-eyed and full of surprise as they woke up on Christmas mornings to witness the magic of Santa Claus.

"You've suffered abuse. One person is dead, and now you're looking at almost a lifetime of jail. None of that is necessary," Judge Smith said to Dixie. "Perhaps, Dixie, your case will make the legislature, which is made up of good people dedicated to public service, take notice and do something to untie the hands of the judges in this state and the parole board in this state. I hope so, and I know your friends and you do, as well."

Lastly, Smith announced that based on section 707.3 of the code of Iowa, Dixie was hereby sentenced to a prison term not to exceed fifty years.

"As I know you're aware," Smith explained, "under the terms of our statutes, you will not be eligible for parole for thirty-five years. The reason for the sentence is the term of the statute. I'm sorry. The reason for the sentence is the statute that we've already discussed, which gives the court no other alternative."

At 9:13 a.m. Smith concluded his remarks to Dixie by saying, "Good luck to you."

Jailers approached Dixie and escorted her back to jail.

Based on Iowa's one-size-fits-all murder sentencing laws, Dixie received a standard fifty-year prison term for second-degree murder. Dixie, almost thirty-seven, would theoretically be more than seventy-one years old before she even became eligible for parole while in prison.

Shortly after her sentence, her lawyer, Greg Steensland, organized a press conference. Throngs of reporters from across Iowa and Nebraska converged upon the small-town Shelby County Jail in downtown Harlan for one lasting and memorable interview with Dixie before she started her new life as a state of Iowa prisoner.

With the cameras rolling, Dixie wore her orange jail jumpsuit and she made the news media event a treat for every journalist who made the jaunt to Harlan, Iowa. She did not provide dull and boring sound bites. No way. She unloaded her true feelings about her worthless husband.

Omaha's NBC television affiliate, WOWT, headlined their story, "Dixie Stands Her Ground." She was defiant and expressed little regret for taking the life of her husband. She seemed to take her second-degree murder conviction in stride.

"I shouldn't have done what I did. But, do I feel I was justified? Yes I do. And, if I was in the same circumstances, would I do it again? Yes, I would," Dixie was quoted by WOWT.

In the aftermath, Dixie's mandatory fifty-year prison sentence continued to capture more attention nationwide.

The Miami Herald's nationally syndicated columnist Leonard Pitts Jr. took a strong interest in the murder conviction of Dixie Shanahan. Pitts devoted a full column on May 27, 2004, to the small-town western Iowa case, headlined "Twice abused, first by husband, then by the court."

"The point is, even if you accept the prosecution's theory of the crime, this sentence is not justice," Pitts wrote. "Not even close. … Like the zero tolerance school policies they resemble, mandatory sentencing guidelines leave (little) room for compassion or common sense. And you have to wonder how many more of these tragic absurdities it will take before legislators concede the obvious: these are awful laws."

Chapter 20 — Dixie's Next Decade

Shortly after Dixie's final press conference at her local jail, the Iowa Department of Corrections took control of Dixie Shanahan's life.

From Harlan, Iowa, it's a two-hour drive east, along Interstate 80, to get to Mitchellville. The small community about twenty miles northeast of Des Moines is the home of the Iowa Correctional Institution for Women.

This was where Dixie was on track to spend anywhere from the next thirty-five to fifty years of her dreadful and disastrous life, thanks to Iowa's no-nonsense, get-tough-on-crime, mandatory-minimum prison-sentencing laws. In prison, you're an inmate number and not a name.

Dixie's new prison number became 0808771.

When Dixie got to Mitchellville, she was one of roughly six hundred female inmates who lived under the thumb of the Iowa women's prison system. The prison buildings were vastly outdated. Some of the structures dated back to the early 1930s. An October 2013 article in The Des Moines Register noted that Mitchellville's inmates were quite accustomed to leaky roofs, lack of air-conditioning, and a bad heating system during the harsh Midwestern winter months.

Not long after Dixie's arrival in 2004 in Mitchellville, she got off to a bad start. Prison guards could care less whether Dixie got hosed by Iowa's stiff and inflexible sentencing laws. They were not interested in hearing her sob stories about her lousy and ruthless husband, Scott. Prison life is about obeying the rules and following orders. In July of 2004, Dixie was busted by the prison guards for unauthorized possession of cigarettes.

Since May 2004, Dixie Shanahan has remained in Mitchellville, Iowa, where she continues to serve out her prison term for second-degree murder at the Iowa Correctional Institute for Women. Photo courtesy of Iowa Department of Corrections

That October, Dixie received at least five more separate disciplinary infractions. She had stolen markers and medications from other inmates and the prison staff, according to her disciplinary sheet. Her infractions included being disobedient of a lawful order, theft, abuse of medication, unauthorized possession/exchange, plus safety and sanitation violations.

On the plus side, Dixie made it through 2005 without a single violation.

In April of 2006, the Iowa Supreme Court finished its analysis of Dixie's appeal of her second-degree murder conviction. The court rejected her appeal in convincing fashion.

"We find no error in the district court's rulings with respect to the motion to suppress, motion for judgment of acquittal, and motion for new trial," the ruling stated.

The following month, Dixie was busted for sneaking an apple out of the women's prison dining hall when she was not supposed to do that.

That July of 2006, as a reporter for the Omaha World-Herald newspaper, I made the two-and-a-half hour drive from Omaha to Des Moines to cover Dixie Shanahan's inaugural hearing before the Iowa Parole Board. More than two years had elapsed since I had covered Dixie's famous murder trial. The hearing before the Iowa Board of Parole marked Dixie's first crack at winning a sentence modification. Nobody in the newsroom knew what to expect, and some of my colleagues predicted that Dixie stood an excellent chance at being set free.

But, it soon became apparent how things would go down.

Dixie, age thirty-eight, appeared by a video teleconferencing feed from the Iowa women's prison in Mitchellville. She remained married to Jeffrey Duty, the same man she began a courtship with during the Memorial Day weekend of 2003. With Scott dead and Dixie in prison, Jeff Duty continued to reside in Dixie's old house in Defiance.

The Iowa Department of Corrections had urged the parole board not to grant Dixie a reduced sentence. Prison officials noted Dixie's bad attitude at times and her disregard for prison rules.

During the live hearing, parole board member Barbara Binnie grilled Dixie about why she had passed up "the plea bargain of a lifetime" when offered a chance to plead guilty to voluntary manslaughter.

"Did you think if you went to trial, everyone would say, 'Poor Dixie, let's set her free?'" Binnie asked the convict, as reported in my newspaper article for the Omaha World-Herald. "You did not take that plea deal because rules don't apply to Dixie Shanahan. She can do whatever she wants. That's going to have to change."

Dixie gave her best shot at persuading the five-member parole board to give her a reduced prison sentence.

"I feel everyone deserves a second chance, and I feel my kids need their mother," Dixie told them.

But Dixie's hearing turned into a nightmare for her. In fact, she would have been much better off not even petitioning the parole board barely two years into her prison sentence for second-degree murder.

Parole Board Chairwoman Elizabeth Robinson scolded Dixie on a number of occasions during the hearing.

Robinson was not sympathetic toward Dixie in the least.

"The message you sent to those children and other battered women is cruel, cruel, cruel," Robinson was quoted in my article. "I've smelled dead animals before. I can't even imagine what it smelled liked."

When your board of parole hearing is focused on the stench of your dead husband's rotting body of fourteen months, things are not very promising.

"There was no smell," Dixie clarified. "There were towels underneath the door."

Not surprisingly, the Iowa Board of Parole was not moved by the fact that Dixie had spread a towel under the door to hide the odors.

Dixie's request for a sentence commutation was rejected in a unanimous five-to-zero vote. In a nutshell, the parole board had denounced Dixie for letting her husband's body rot in the bedroom as

Dixie continued to reside there and raise her three children in the process.

* * *

Dixie's first glimmer of hope arrived in January of 2007, thanks to the intervention of Iowa Governor Tom Vilsack, who was on the verge of leaving office.

After weighing how to handle Dixie's request for a sentence commutation, Vilsack decided not to rubber stamp his board of parole's five-to-zero recommendation. But ever the crafty politician, Vilsack stopped short of going over the goal line for the touchdown. Iowa's governor did not simply release Dixie from prison. Rather, he skillfully reduced her mandatory minimum sentence from seventy percent to twenty percent before she was eligible for parole.

In essence, Dixie would become eligible for parole around April 21, 2014.

"The result I arrive at today strikes a balance between the views of those who believe the sentence was appropriate and those who believe Ms. Duty should not be punished at all," the governor stated in a letter to parole board chairwoman Elizabeth Robinson.

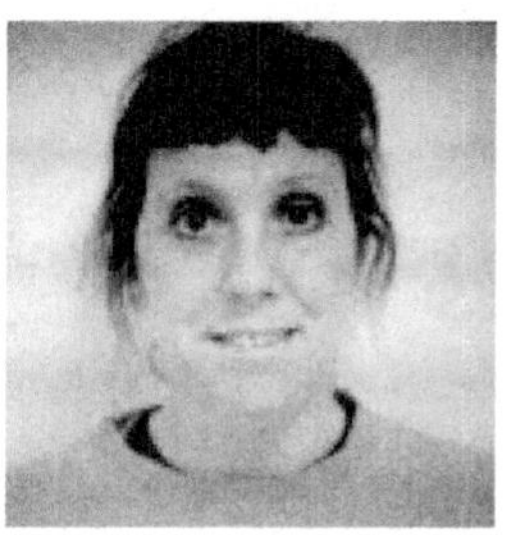

Dixie Shanahan, now age 47, has spent more than a decade in prison for killing her husband, Scott Shanahan. In 2014, the Iowa Board of Parole rejected Dixie's bid for early release from prison. She will be eligible for another parole board hearing sometime in 2015. Photo courtesy of Iowa Department of Corrections

The governor referred to Dixie in his public statements by her new married surname of Duty.

"To be clear, Dixie's sentence shall remain a term of fifty years, but the mandatory minimum sentence is reduced from thirty-five to ten years," Vilsack pointed out.

And with that, Vilsack's role in the Dixie Shanahan case was over.

As Dixie remained in prison, Vilsack, a popular Democrat, became one of the most important politicians in the Beltway when newly elected U.S. President Barack Obama appointed him as his U.S. Secretary of Agriculture.

At the time of Vilsack's decision, Dixie's former trial lawyer, Greg Steensland, mentioned that Dixie finally had a reason to feel optimistic about her situation.

"There's now light at the end of the tunnel," Steensland was quoted in my article for the Omaha World-Herald.

Sure, there might have been a flicker of light for Dixie, but her tunnel to get out of prison remained as a dark as an underground cave.

Chapter 21 — Denial

Former Iowa Governor Tom Vilsack's sentence commutation set the stage for Dixie Shanahan's possible release from custody after serving roughly ten years of her fifty-year prison sentence. But, Dixie's attitude mattered. She needed to remain on her best behavior in the eyes of Iowa's strict-and-rigid prison system. After all, Dixie was one of Iowa's most high-profile female prisoners. And plus, she had not exactly been convicted of shoplifting candy at the gas station. She was in prison after a jury of her peers found her guilty of second-degree murder.

In 2014, Dixie had celebrated a somber milestone. She had spent an entire decade locked up and housed away from society. She was approaching her forty-seventh birthday. The last time she was free and out in society, her children were ages about eight, six, and one. In 2014, her three children were a full ten years older, a lot taller, and far, far away from her. They lived with relatives in Texas after the Iowa courts had formally revoked Dixie's legal parental rights around 2007.

In June of 2014, the Iowa Board of Parole reviewed her case for the first time since Vilsack had commuted the mandatory minimum portion of her sentence to make her eligible for parole. But if Dixie assumed that the Iowa Department of Corrections was about to open up the prison gates at Mitchellville and send her off with a cake and balloons and a big farewell send-off, well, Dixie was badly mistaken.

For starters, Dixie had not been a model prisoner. She had lots of blemishes on her disciplinary record.

In 2010, she received another disciplinary infraction for having unauthorized property in her possession. In 2011, she received four separate infractions all stemming from the same incident. As a consequence, she was reprimanded for giving false statements, obstructive/disruptive behavior, refusal or failing to work, and also unauthorized possession/exchange.

Dixie's bubble-burst came on June 19, 2014. That was the day the Iowa Board of Parole flatly denied her bid for parole. Dixie was quite deflated. She believed she had served enough hard time, now more than a decade, to warrant her release back into society.

But, that was not so.

"Your case will be reviewed again at or before the date scheduled for your next annual review," Iowa Board of Parole Chairman John Hodges notified Dixie in a letter denying her request for parole.

Dixie's official rejection letter noted the underlying reason for denying her bid for parole.

"The seriousness of your crime or your criminal history suggests to the Board you have not yet served enough time to warrant an early release," the letter read. "The Board commends your positive efforts and wants to see you continue to have a positive outlook and perspective. Positive efforts and behavior indicate you may be able and willing to fulfill the obligations of a law-abiding citizen."

In response, Dixie quickly submitted a page-long typed letter back to the Iowa Board of Parole, dated June 30, 2014. She appealed to the board members to reconsider their earlier decision.

"I believe that the decision is based on only a small number of factors of available case information, ignoring other seemingly relevant factors," Dixie wrote in her appeal letter. "I have a home to go to, a vehicle, a job, support from the community, family, and friends … everything that would make a successful person to parole. I also have the backing of the place that I have been for the last ten years. I have done everything to make my re-entry a successful one."

On July 9, 2014, John Hodges, the parole board chairman, wrote Dixie back. Her plea had left him unmoved.

His mind was unchanged.

"After a review of your request for reconsideration on July 8, 2014, the Board has agreed that no modification will be made of the original decision in your case," Hodges notified Dixie. "You will be screened again at or before your next scheduled review date. This is the final decision in this matter."

* * *

This year, 2015, marks Dixie's eleventh full year at the Iowa Correctional Institution for Women in Polk County. The town of Mitchellville is surrounded by a swath of cornfields. The women's prison in Mitchellville is encompassed by a sixteen-foot-high chain-link fence wrapped with razor wire.

As it stands today, the average prison sentence for a female convict assigned to Mitchellville is about fifteen years. Dixie is serving out a fifty-year term. The average female inmate is in her mid-thirties. Dixie is approaching her late-forties. In October 2013, the state of Iowa opened a brand new sixty-eight-million-dollar Iowa women's prison in Mitchellville. The new prison was a tremendous upgrade from the old brick-and-mortar facility where Dixie previously resided in Mitchellville.

Roughly six hundred female offenders live in dormitory-style housing units or cell blocks. Many of the women prisoners at the new top-of-the-line prison facility are serving time for drug convictions, theft, and forgery crimes. About three dozen women are serving life sentences for first-degree murder. Dixie is one of nearly twenty female inmates who are serving prison terms for second-degree murder. Iowa's women's prison also offers a number of programs for inmates such as Dixie Shanahan to help them prepare for eventual re-entry into society. Some of the prison's programs include decision-making skills, thinking patterns, self-esteem, parenting, domestic violence, interpersonal relationships, career assessment and exploration, and health education, according to the prison's website.

These days, Dixie and her fellow female inmates continue to acclimate to their new-and-improved digs. In addition, Dixie still remains married to Jeff Duty, and he continues to reside in her old house in Defiance, the same house that once belonged to Scott Shanahan. The same house that Dixie used to store the body of her previous husband, Scott Shanahan. The same house that was the site of one of western Iowa's most peculiar murders.

As for Scott Shanahan, he has a grave in Iowa with a cross across the top of his tombstone to memorialize his time on earth. Like a lot of the happenings in this bizarre small-town murder case, there is one glaring error on Scott's tombstone.

Scott Shanahan's grave lists his official date of death as being October 20, 2003. But that was the date when Shelby County Sheriff Gene Cavenaugh and his tenacious law enforcement crew stumbled onto Scott's human remains in the back northeast corner bedroom. In reality, Scott was dead for at least fourteen months.

He most likely died before Labor Day in 2002.

And that's the really goofy thing about this weird Iowa murder case. Nobody quite knows precisely what time and day Scott Shanahan was murdered. He may have died on August 30, 2002, but it's entirely possible he was killed during the night as early as August 26, 2002.

"It was a strange, strange case," Cavenaugh told me in a 2014 interview. "It was a sad situation where someone had to die, someone had to go to prison, and they lost their children. In hindsight, if she would have told us and said, 'I shot Scott and killed him,' during the very beginning and had been truthful with us at the outset, I think she would have probably got a less sentence, probably a lot less than fifty years."

* * *

These days, some of the key faces who were involved in the historic and monumental small-town Iowa murder case have moved on.

Thoman, the one-man ironman prosecution team, who successfully prosecuted Dixie Shanahan for murder, retired at the end of 2013 after a long and distinguished career with the Iowa Attorney General's Office.

Iowa Fourth Judicial District Judge Charles Smith III, who presided over the jury trial and sentenced Dixie, also has since retired from the bench in southwestern Iowa.

On the other spectrum, Dixie's two court-appointed public defenders out of Council Bluffs, Greg Steensland and Charles Fagan, both are now judges in southwestern Iowa. Susan Christensen no longer works as an assistant Shelby County attorney because she also wears a long black robe as an Iowa judge, just like her brother, Jeff Larson, who has been a judge since 2003.

Cavenaugh retired as the Shelby County sheriff on December 31, 2008. Today, he works as the county's Veterans Affairs Commission director. His longtime and highly capable chief deputy sheriff, Mark Hervey, has served as Shelby County's sheriff since 2009.

Like his predecessor, Hervey is equally confident that Dixie would not still be doing hard time if she had notified law enforcement rather quickly about the deadly shooting.

"I believe in my heart that she would have gotten little or nothing out of this," Hervey told me in a recent interview. "I am sure the penalties would have been a lot less than what it ended up being."

As it stands, the thirty-acre plot of Iowa state government property in Mitchellville, not the serene, tree-lined neighborhood ranch with the two-acre yard on Third Avenue in Defiance, likely will remain Dixie Shanahan's permanent mailing address for the indefinite future.

"She rolled the dice," Hervey added. "There was a lot of sympathy in the community for her. Honestly, I would not have been surprised if they had come back with a not-guilty verdict."

Both the current and former sheriffs of Shelby County received letters in the mail from Dixie Shanahan in anticipation of her noteworthy June 2014 hearing before the Iowa Board of Parole. In her personalized letter to the current sheriff, she respectfully asked Hervey to write a letter to the Iowa Board of Parole on her behalf.

"I just did not respond," Hervey told me.

Hervey said it is not his role to lobby on behalf of convicted prisoners on whether the parole board should commute their sentences or award them early release. In Dixie's case, a jury of twelve citizens heard the evidence and convicted Dixie of second-degree murder. She received a lengthy prison sentence, based on Iowa's sentencing guidelines for that particular crime.

"I investigated the case, the jury made its decision, and the court handed the sentence down," Hervey said. "We'll let the legal system run its course. It's a parole board decision, not mine."

Likewise, Cavenaugh told me he decided not to take sides in Dixie's parole board matter, as well.

* * *

Occasionally, smaller law enforcement agencies get a bad rap for acting unprofessional and being improperly trained and overmatched when it comes to handling high-profile criminal cases, notably murders. For a variety of reasons, some small-town murders turn into frustrating, dead-end cold cases because those police departments become overwhelmed or were ill-equipped to track down the unknown perpetrator or perpetrators.

The missing person case of Scott J. Shanahan had a drastically different outcome, and it's an excellent case study of a small-town criminal case in a Midwestern community that came together very quickly, once the cops were made aware of something amiss in Defiance.

Those law enforcement officials who had a role in investigating the case and bringing Dixie Shanahan to justice deserve to be commended.

The Shelby County Sheriff's Office in Harlan, Iowa, an agency with fewer than ten sworn deputies, worked closely with the Iowa Division of Criminal Investigation to bring finality to the odd and hideous case. There were no bumbling mistakes or errors. The case was put together nicely.

The Shelby County Sheriff's Office was first notified of Scott's disappearance toward the latter part of summer in 2003. By the middle of that October, the agency and DCI had established sufficient probable cause to obtain a legal search warrant to enter Scott and Dixie's home. In there, Scott's remains were found. Scott's gruesome death was ruled to be a homicide, and his wife, Dixie, was immediately arrested for murder. The crime scene was preserved. The autopsy revealed that Scott suffered a shotgun shell wound through the back of his skull.

"It was excellent teamwork with an excellent conclusion," Hervey said. "There was good old-fashioned police work. Different agencies came together, the Shelby County Sheriff's Office and the DCI, and we got a conviction. We worked well together and did a lot of follow up, and I was proud of it. I really was."

Of particular note, Hervey complimented his former boss, Gene Cavenaugh. The retired longtime Iowa sheriff spearheaded the investigation and deserved most of the accolades for solving the mystery.

Gene Cavenaugh (seated), was the long-time sheriff of ShelbyCounty, Iowa, who spearheaded the missing person investigation into thewhereabouts of Scott Shanahan. Mark Hervey (standing), the chief deputysheriff at the time, was also instrumental in the investigation. Photo courtesy of The Harlan Newspapers

"Gene did a lot of the legwork," Hervey said. "It was somewhat his case, and I was honored to be a part of it, assisting in it."

True, Cavenaugh did not simply shrug off the disappearance of Scott Shanahan when he first got wind of the matter. He took the case seriously from day one, even though the case involved a missing adult male. The easy thing to do was to completely brush off the concerned tipster's suggestion. After all, men and women in their thirties and forties have been known to move around, desert their spouses, pick up and leave their families because they want to start over and rediscover their life in a faraway, distant place.

But, as far as Sheriff Cavenaugh was concerned, that did not sound like Scott Shanahan.

Even when the sheriff was hot on the missing person's trail, he came to a fork in the road. If the sheriff had taken the wrong path, he might have dropped the missing person investigation altogether. After all, there was that man from Irwin, Iowa, who insisted that he was sure he had seen Scott Shanahan in the McDonald's restaurant parking lot during the spring of 2003 — which would have been several months after Scott was obviously dead from a gunshot wound to the head.

It's quite morbid to think about it, but without the swift sheriff's intervention, it's possible that Scott's decomposed remains might still be under the covers of his bed to this very day.

"Once we found out Dixie was selling off his tools and cars, well, if Scott was alive and in Iowa, she'd not have done that. She would be too afraid of him," Cavenaugh said during a 2014 interview. "I just felt like something was not right here, and our fears were this was foul play. We just did not know the why and the how. The story we were told had not panned out. I think the people in Defiance felt like something had happened to Scott also."

Besides the Shelby County Sheriff's Office and the Iowa DCI, Assistant Attorney General Charles Thoman from Sioux City deserves a ton of credit for securing Dixie's conviction on the second-degree murder count.

"Chuck did an excellent job," Hervey said.

Contrary to the defendant's theme during her murder trial, Sheriff Hervey told me that it's his experience that there are lots of resources available for people who find themselves as victims of domestic abuse, even in smaller, rural areas such as Shelby County, Iowa, which has less than thirteen thousand residents scattered across about a dozen different communities and tiny towns.

In 2009, Mark Hervey succeeded Gene Cavenaugh as sheriff of Shelby County, Iowa. Hervey is extremely proud of his small-town law enforcement agency's role in solving the baffling disappearance of Scott Shanahan. Photo courtesy of Shelby County Sheriff's Office

Finally, Hervey hopes he never has to investigate another brutal crime that ends up the way the Dixie and Scott Shanahan case turned out.

"There are tools out there for women," Hervey said during the 2014 interview. "There are laws, protection orders, shelters, if they take advantage of it. Every female individual is different, and some take advantage of (the resources available) and some elect to stay in the abusive relationship."

Dixie chose to ignore the help and stay in her abusive relationship. Then, she turned into a murderer.

* * *

The most recent headshot on file for Iowa state prisoner number 0808771 shows Dixie Shanahan wearing a gray sweatshirt. Her hair is dark brown. She is smiling in her prison photo.

Readers of this book will certainly draw their own conclusions as to whether Dixie has done enough hard time for her crime and whether she deserves to be set free or should stay in prison.

Iowa Department of Corrections policies prohibit the public release of specific work assignments for Dixie Shanahan and other state prisoners. However, many prisoners are typically assigned to work for Prison Industries, which often consists of more manufacturing and industrial type of work. Others receive what's known as an institutional assignment. Those jobs may include duties in a kitchen, laundry, cleaning, and maintenance. Jobs inside the prison typically pay between twenty-seven cents to fifty-six cents per hour. Those inmates lucky enough to be assigned to Prison Industries make fifty-eight to eighty-seven cents per hour.

It's worth pointing out that Dixie has now served more time in prison than if she had accepted the prosecution's offer to plead guilty to voluntary manslaughter in April of 2004.

Reflecting on the case recently, retired Judge Smith

noted that several Iowa lawmakers had commented in the news media about how they had intended to forge ahead with efforts to overhaul Iowa's mandatory-minimum sentencing laws to ensure that a situation such as Dixie Shanahan's never happened again. That was back around 2004. It turns out that nothing ever materialized. Iowa's mandatory-minimum penalties for second-degree murder are still the same today as they were more than a decade ago.

Smith said the lack of follow-through by either political party in Iowa should not be a shock to anybody.

"I am not surprised," he said. "But I am disappointed."

Unfortunately, Smith said, he expects Iowa's mandatory minimum prison terms will remain in place for a long time. There is no reason for optimism that Iowa's lawmakers will enact measures to give their state's judges more latitude, especially in second-degree murder cases, where quite a number of mitigating factors might be a pivotal factor for the court and the judge to consider at the sentencing.

"I don't see it happening," Smith said during the 2014 interview. "I think the right thing to do is examine it. (But,) who wants to be portrayed as being soft on crime in the eyes of the voters?"

Smith believes that Dixie will be given early release from the Iowa board of parole, but he is not sure if that should happen in the near future or several years down the road.

"I would assume she will get paroled," Smith told me. "She had excellent representation, and they did everything they could to help her."

* * *

The mission statement of the Iowa Correctional Institution for Women proclaims on its website: "As role models, we empower women to change their lives and return to the community as healthier productive citizens."

The odds of Dixie committing any more crimes that would land her back inside the Iowa women's prison are extraordinarily low. And yet, Dixie stands a good chance of remaining a burden for the Iowa state taxpayers for many more years as she continues to plug along and pay back her debt to society behind the tall chain-link fence draped with razor wire at the Iowa Correctional Institution for Women in Mitchellville.

Maybe she will receive her parole this year in 2015 or sometime during the tenure of current conservative Republican Governor Terry Branstad. In November 2014, Branstad just won an overwhelming re-election to serve another four-year term. Then again, Dixie's parole may happen thirty years from now when she has gray hair and is in her late-seventies.

"She's still there (in Mitchellville)," Cavenaugh said. "There is no doubt that at some point she will get out, and I think she will move back to Defiance and live in that same house. I think if she has turned her life around and learned from what she did, I fully expect she will get out at some time — since she's in for fifty years."

It kind of goes without saying, but it needs to be said anyway: Dixie Shanahan had an incredibly bad streak of luck during her dysfunctional life, and that misfortune traces all the way back to her childhood. As a grown adult, virtually all of her important decisions have gone disastrous for her. With that kind of luck, readers who are sympathetic to Dixie's cause should guard against being overly optimistic about Dixie's prospects of being granted parole in Iowa anytime really soon.

In the eyes of Iowa's justice system, Dixie Shanahan is convicted of MURDER — second degree. She is someone who committed a rather violent, serious offense.

Thoman, the five-star prosecutor who secured Dixie's murder conviction, said one of his lasting impressions of the Iowa murder case was the large degree of support that Dixie had gained from a number of domestic violence groups.

Their discontent was obvious before, during, and after Dixie's murder trial.

"There seemed to be a consensus among many of these people that because she was physically and emotionally abused by Scott Shanahan many times throughout their marriage, this gave defendant Shanahan a green light to take Scott's life," Thoman told me.

"It was as if I was persecuting an innocent victim, instead of a person charged with first-degree murder. As a prosecutor, I had always respected the domestic violence advocates. I was surprised by their sometimes open hostility toward this prosecution."

Thoman happens to have a strong opinion on the topic of Dixie Shanahan being granted parole from Mitchellville.

"I am very much against any parole for Dixie Shanahan," Thoman said. "She shot a sleeping man in the back of the head. That, in my mind, is cold-blooded murder. Had she shown some remorse, some regret, then I might feel differently.

"In that press conference, she said that given the opportunity she would do it again. That statement opens a window into her soul, and it is the soul of a murderer, not a victim."

Thank you for reading Dixie's Last Stand. I hope you enjoyed it as much as I enjoyed writing it. If you did like it then I'd appreciate it if you provided an honest review at http://wildbluepress.com/DixieReviews.

You can sign up for advance notice of new releases at: http://wildbluepress.com/AdvanceNotice

Thank you for your interest in my books,

John Ferak

See the Next Page for More about No Stone Unturned

Check out more True CRIME and Crime Fiction from WildBlue Press

www.WildBluePress.com

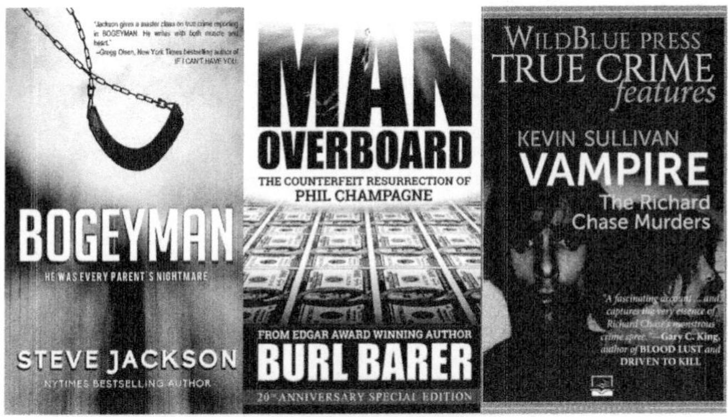

Go to WildBluePress.com to sign up for our newsletter!

By subscribing to our newsletter you'll get *advance notice* of all new releases as well as notifications of all special offers. And you'll be registered for our monthly chance to win a **FREE collection of our eBooks and/or audio books** to some lucky fan who has posted an honest review of our one of our books/eBooks/audio books on Amazon, Itunes and GoodReads.

Please feel free to check out more True CRIME books by our friends at

www.RJPARKERPUBLISHING.com

Printed in Great Britain
by Amazon

57728353R00122